BABY LOVE

Cuddly Knits
for Wee Ones

CATHERINE BOUQUEREL

 sixth&springbooks
NEW YORK

For my ninety-year-old mother, who still takes much pleasure
in knitting for the new babies in our family.

Thanks to Sonia and Fabrice for their fabulous photos,
and to all the team at Le Temps Apprivoisé.

sixth&springbooks

161 Avenue of the Americas,
New York, New York 10013
sixthandspringbooks.com

FOR SIXTH&SPRING BOOKS
Editorial Director
JOY AQUILINO

Senior Editor
MICHELLE BREDESON

Art Director
DIANE LAMPHRON

Yarn Editors
RENÉE LORION, CHRISTINA BEHNKE

Associate Editor
ALEXANDRA JOINNIDES

Vice President, Publisher
TRISHA MALCOLM

Creative Director
JOE VIOR

Production Manager
DAVID JOINNIDES

President
ART JOINNIDES

FOR LTA
Editorial Director
VALÉRIE GENDREAU

Editor
ISABELLE RIENER

Proofreaders
ÉVA DOLOWSKI, VÉRONIQUE LINART

Graphic Design
ANNE BÉNOLIEL-DEFRÉVILLE

Layout
COLINE DE GRAAFF

Photography
FABRICE BESSE

Stylist
SONIA ROY

ISBN: 978-1-936096-39-8

Library of Congress Control Number: 2012932051

Translation by Rosemary Perkins

1 3 5 7 9 10 8 6 4 2

First English Edition

PRINTED IN CHINA

Preface

For this book I wanted to come up with some cute patterns for the very youngest babies, including the extra-early arrivals. Moms and grandmoms will be able to make these adorable outfits very quickly and give the littlest ones a wardrobe "just like the big kids."

I'm sure you'll want to keep these darling knits to remind yourself, one day, that your babies were Lilliputians before they grew up to be giants!

I hope you'll enjoy making these knit gifts for your little baby-loves as much as I enjoyed creating them.

Berquerel

Contents

Materials and tips

Materials

* **Yarns** You'll use yarns in a variety of weights and fibers, including wool, wool blends, cotton, and acrylic. If you want to substitute yarns, find one with the same yarn weight number (indicated in the Materials list of each pattern) and gauge.

* **Knitting needles:** The patterns in this book were knitted with needles in the following sizes: 2 (2.75mm), 3 (3.25mm), 4 (3.5mm), 6 (4mm), 7 (4.5mm), 8 (5mm), 9 (5.5mm), and 10 (6mm).

* **Trimmings** The right trimming adds an elegant, unique touch to your booties; try ribbons, beads, and fancy buttons.

Tips

* **When a single number of rows is given in a pattern,** it applies to both sizes.

* **To start a ball of yarn**
Pull on the end of yarn that's tucked inside, so the yarn unwinds neatly without raveling. When joining a new ball, start at the beginning of a row. If you find a knot in the yarn, work back to the beginning of the row, cut the yarn after the knot, and rework the row.

* **For an even finish**
If you're a beginner, it's a good idea to practice on a few small, straight projects, such as a doll's scarf or a coverlet for a bassinet. Make sure that the yarn is neither too taut nor too loose, so that the stitches slip easily over the needles.

* **For a neat edge**
Always pull the first stitch of a row a little tighter; this will keep the work from stretching.

* **To pick up a dropped stitch**
Pass a crochet hook through the dropped stitch, then hook the horizontal strand just above the dropped stitch and pass it through the stitch on the hook. Repeat through as many rows as necessary, and slip the final loop on to the left-hand needle.

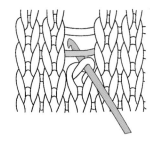

ABBREVIATIONS

Use of abbreviations makes it faster and easier to follow the instructions.

beg	beginning	p	purl
ch st	chain stitch	psso	pass sl st over
cont	continue	rep	repeat
dc	double crochet	rnd	round
dec	decrease	RS	right side
dpn(s)	double-pointed needle(s)	sc	single crochet
		SKP	single decrease
foll	following/ follows	SK2P or S2KP	double decrease
4-st RC	4-stitch right (back) cable	sl	slip
		sl st	slip stitch
inc	increase	st(s)	stitch(es)
k	knit	St st	stockinette stitch
k1-b	knit 1 in the row below		
		tog	together
k2tog	knit 2 stitches together	WS	wrong side
lp(s)	loop(s)	yo	yarn over

6

Knitting basics

CASTING ON

1. Allowing a good length of yarn (about 3 times the intended width), form a slip knot and insert a needle through the central loop.
2. Wind the yarn around your left thumb, keeping the needle in your right hand.
3. Insert the needle under the loop around your left thumb; using your left hand, flip the yarn (that's coming from the ball) over the tip of the needle and pull the yarn toward you.
4. Pass the loop over the tip of the needle.
5. Gently pull the yarn on the left downward: You've formed a stitch on the needle.

Repeat from step 2 until you have the number of stitches required to cast on for the pattern.

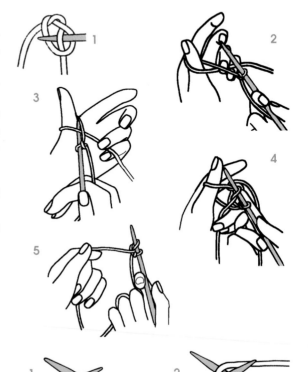

KNIT STITCH

Keep the yarn at the back of the work.

1. Insert the right-hand needle through the stitch from left to right, passing under the left-hand needle.
2. Pass the yarn over the right-hand needle from bottom to top.
3. Draw the right-hand needle with the loop back through the stitch, then over the left-hand-needle.
4. Slip the loop off the left-hand needle: the new stitch is now on the right-hand needle.
5. Repeat steps 1–4 for each stitch. At the end of the row, all the stitches will be on the right-hand needle.

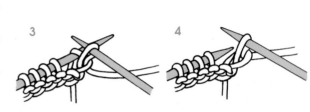

TIP

For a neat fabric, keep an even tension and always pull the yarn in the same direction. The stitches should slide easily on the needles without being too loose.

PURL STITCH

Keep the yarn in front of the work.

1. Insert the right-hand needle through the first stitch from right to left, toward front of work.
2. Pass the yarn over the right-hand needle.
3. Draw the right-hand needle through the stitch, pulling slightly to the right.
4. Slip the loop off the left-hand needle; the new stitch is on the right-hand needle.
5. Repeat steps 1–4 for each stitch. At the end of the row, all the stitches will be on the right-hand needle.

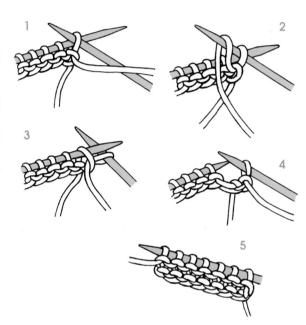

STOCKINETTE STITCH

Row 1 Knit (each stitch forms a V).
Row 2 Purl (each stitch forms a little horizontal bar).
Repeat these 2 rows.

REVERSE STOCKINETTE STITCH

Row 1 Purl (each stitch forms a little horizontal bar).
Row 2 Knit (each stitch forms a V).
Repeat these 2 rows.

GARTER STITCH

Knit every row.

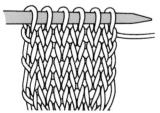 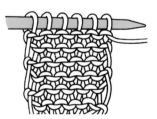 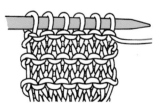

K1, P1 RIB
Over an odd number of stitches:
Row 1 *K1, p1, rep from * to end of row, ending with k1.
Row 2 *P1, k1, rep from * to end of row, ending with p1.
Repeat row 2 for k1, p1 rib.

K2, P2 RIB
Over a multiple of 4 stitches plus 2:
Row 1 *K2, p2, rep from * to end of row.
Row 2 Knit the knit stitches, purl the purl stitches.
Repeat row 2 for k2, p2 rib.

SLIP STITCH
Slip a stitch from the left-hand needle onto the right-hand needle without working it.

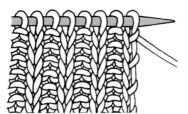

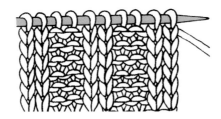

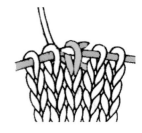

P2, K1 RIB
Row 1 *P2, k1, rep from * to end of row.
Row 2 K the knit stitches, p the purl stitches.
Repeat row 2 for p2, k1 rib.

FISHERMAN'S RIB
Row 1 Knit.
Row 2 K1, * p1, k1-b (insert needle into next st 1 row below the row you're working, knit through this stitch) *, rep from * to * until 2 sts remain, p1, k1. Rep these 2 rows.

10

SEED STITCH
Over an odd number of stitches:
Row 1 *K1, p1, repeat from *, ending with k1.
Rep row 1 for seed st.

MOSS STITCH
Row 1 *K1, p1, rep from * to end.
Row 2 K the knit stitches, p the purl stitches.
Row 3 *P1, k1, rep from * to end.
Row 4 K the knit stitches, p the purl stitches.
Rep these 4 rows.

DOUBLE DECREASE (S2KP)
Slip the first 2 stitches as if to knit, knit the next st. Using the left-hand needle, pick up the 2 slipped stitches and pass them over the stitch you just worked. You now have 2 fewer stitches.

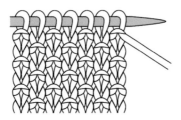

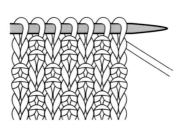

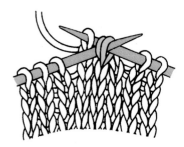

KNIT 2 TOGETHER
(K2TOG)

Insert the right-hand needle into the next two stitches as if to knit. Pass the yarn over the right-hand needle, draw the loop through both stitches, and slip both stitches off the left-hand needle. You now have 1 less stitch in the row.

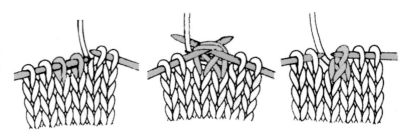

SINGLE DECREASE
(SKP)

Slip a stitch from the left-hand needle to the right-hand needle; knit the next stitch. Using the left-hand needle, pick up the slipped stitch and pass it over the stitch just worked. You now have 1 less stitch in the row.

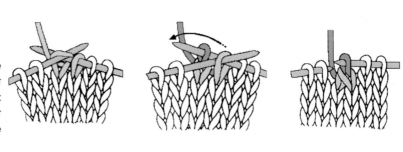

DOUBLE DECREASE
(SK2P)

Slip a stitch from the left-hand needle to the right-hand needle; knit the next 2 stitches together. Using the left-hand needle, pick up the slipped stitch and pass it over the 2 stitches just worked. You now have 2 fewer stitches.

YARN OVER

Between 2 stitches, pass the yarn over the right-hand needle from front to back to form a hole.
Continue according to the instructions to the end of the row.
Next row Work the yarn-over loop as for the other stitches. You now have 1 extra stitch in the row.

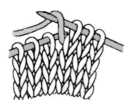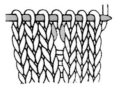

ADDING STITCHES AT ENDS OF ROWS

Form loops by winding the yarn around the needle as many times as you need new stitches.
Work the new stitches according to the instructions.

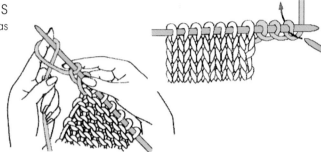

INCREASING 1 OR 2 STITCHES AT THE EDGES

At start of row, * knit 1 or 2, insert tip of right-hand needle under loop between 2 stitches (work through back of loop in order to twist the new st), knit the loop *.
At end of row, when 1 or 2 stitches remain, repeat from * to *, then knit to end.

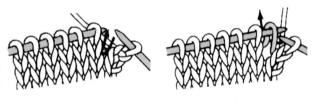

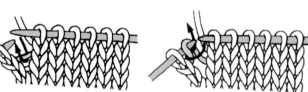

12

DECREASING 1 OR 2 STITCHES FROM THE EDGES

At start of row, knit 1 or 2 sts, work a single decrease as above (SKP).
At end of row, when 3 or 4 stitches remain, knit 2 together, then knit to end.

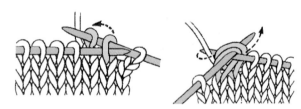

BINDING OFF

To form armholes or necks, or to finish off the work, bind off from right to left.
With right side facing, knit 2, pass the first st over the second, then knit 1, pass the previous st over the one just worked, and so on until you have bound off the number of stitches indicated.
With wrong side facing, work as for right side, but purl instead of knit.

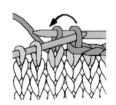

ROUND BUTTONHOLES

This method is ideal for little round buttonholes.
When you have worked the number of stitches indicated, yarn over, knit 2 together, continue to end.
Next row Work the yarn-forward loop as for the other stitches; the little hole will let the button through.

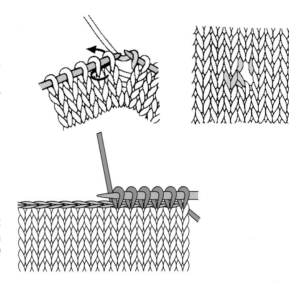

PICKING UP AND KNITTING STITCHES

Working in the direction of the knitting: With yarn at back and right side of work facing, * insert the needle through a stitch in the last row, pass the yarn over the needle as if to knit, draw the loop through the stitch, and repeat from *.

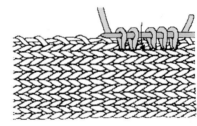

At edge of knitting (ends of rows): With yarn at back and right side of work facing, * insert the needle between the last 2 stitches, pass the yarn over the needle as if to knit, draw the loop through the stitch, and repeat from * in 3 stitches all told in 3 consecutive rows, then skip 1 row and repeat from *.

13

4-ST RIGHT (BACK) CABLE (4-ST RC)

Slip the next 2 stitches onto a cable needle, hold to back. Knit 2, then knit the 2 stitches from the cable needle.

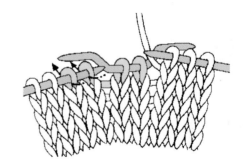

INVISIBLE SEAMS

Work invisible seams with right side facing, between two sections knitted in the same direction, and using a tapestry needle and the same yarn you used for the sections you're joining. Pass the yarn under the horizontal strand between the first and 2nd stitches at the edge of a section, then under the matching strand of the other section; pull firmly to make both sections meet, continue to end. The seam will be invisible.

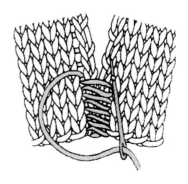

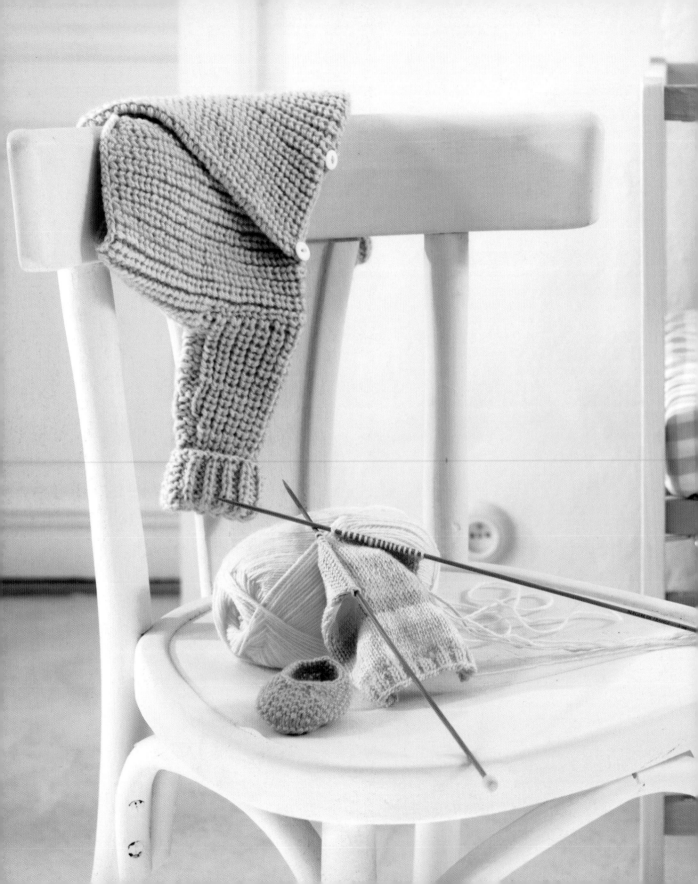

Baby's first pajamas

Fresh white pajamas are perfect for after my bath.

BACK

Beg with the left leg. Using size 2 (2.75mm) needles, cast on 32 (36) sts and work in k2, p2 rib, beg and end row 1 with k3. Cont until left leg measures 1½"/4cm from cast-on edge.

Next row Switch to size 3 (3.25mm) needles and St st, decreasing 5 sts evenly over the course of the row—27 (31) sts. Cont straight in St st until leg measures 4¼ (5)"/10.5 (12.5) cm from cast-on edge.

Next row Shape the crotch as follows: k2, inc 1, work to end. Work 1 row straight. Rep this inc every 2 rows twice—30 (34) sts, then leave the sts on a spare needle. Work the right leg as for the left, reversing the shaping, and, after completing the 3 inc rows, cast on 4 at inner edge, then work across the sts for the left leg—64 (72) sts. Cont straight until back measures 8¾ (9½)"/22 (24)cm from cast-on edge.

Next row K2, k2tog, work until 4 sts remain, SKP, k2. Rep this dec row every 10 (12) rows twice—58 (66) sts. Cont straight until back measures 12 (13½)"/30 (34)cm from cast-on edge, then shape the armholes by binding off 8 sts at beg of next 2 rows—42 (50) sts. Cont straight until back measures 15½ (17¾)"/40 (45)cm from cast-on edge. Bind off.

FRONT

Beg with the right leg. Using size 2 (2.75mm) needles, cast on 32 (36) sts and work in k2, p2 rib, beg and end row 1 with k3. Cont until right leg measures 1½"/4cm from cast-on edge.

Next row Switch to size 3 (3.25mm) needles and St st, decreasing 5 sts evenly over the course of the row—27 (31) sts. Cont straight in St st until leg measures 4¼ (5)"/10.5 (12.5) cm from cast-on edge.

Next row Shape the crotch as follows: K2, inc 1, work to end. Work 1 row straight. Rep this inc every 2 rows twice—30 (34) sts, then leave the sts on a spare needle. Work the left leg as for the right, reversing the shaping, and, after completing the 3 inc rows, cast on 4 at inner edge, then work across the sts for the right leg—64 (72) sts. Cont straight until front measures 7½ (9)"/19 (23)cm from cast-on edge, then shape the opening as follows:

Next row K22 (25), cast on 20 (22) sts—42 (47) sts. Leave the remaining sts on a stitch holder or spare needle.

Cont straight in striped garter st over the newly cast-on sts and in St st over the remaining sts until work measures 8¾ (9½)"/22 (24) cm from cast-on edge.

Next row K2, k2tog, knit to end. Rep this dec row every 10 (12) rows twice. Cont straight until front measures 11¾ (13½)"/30 (34)cm from cast-on edge, then shape the armhole by binding off 8 sts at beg of next RS row—31 (36) sts. Cont straight until front measures 14½ (16)"/37 (41)cm from cast-on edge, at completion of 9th garter st stripe, then shape neck as follows:

Next row With WS facing, bind off 20 (22) sts, work to end—11 (14) sts. Cont straight until front measures 15½ (17¾)"/40 (45)cm from cast-on edge. Bind off remaining sts loosely for shoulder.

Pick up the 42 (47) sts from the holder and work the first 20 (22) sts in striped garter st for the bib and the remaining 22 (25) sts in St st until front measures 8¾ (9½)"/22 (24) cm from cast-on edge.

Next row Work in pat until 4 sts remain, SKP, k2. Rep this dec row every 10 (12) rows twice

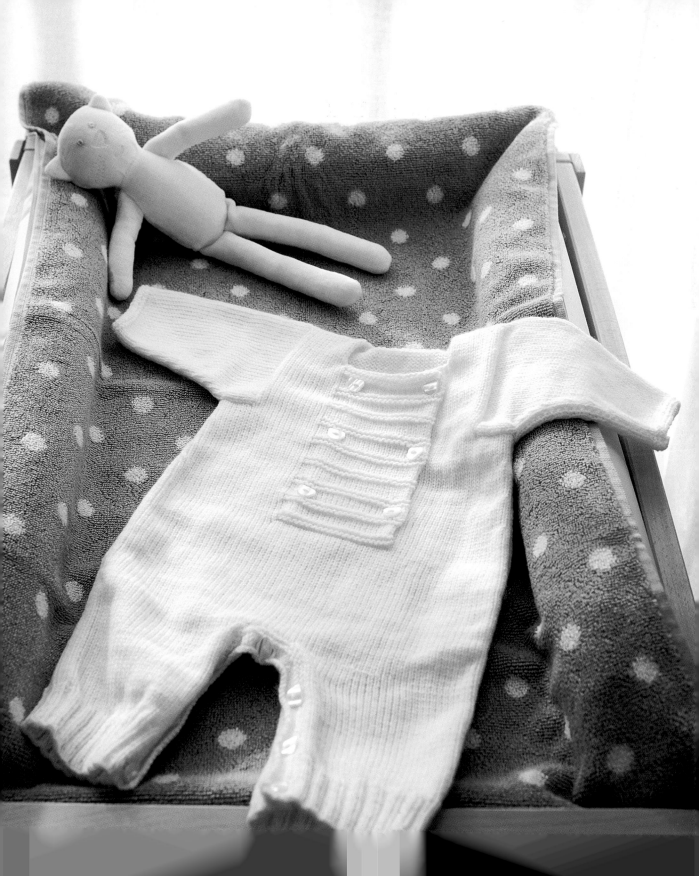

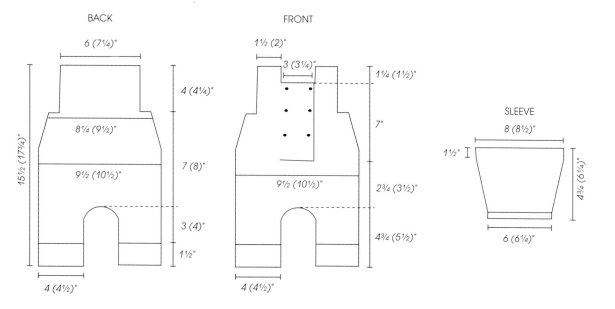

BACK

6 (7¼)"

4 (4¼)"

8¼ (9½)"

15½ (17¾)"

9½ (10½)"

7 (8)"

3 (4)"

1½"

4 (4½)"

FRONT

1½ (2)"

3 (3¼)"

1¼ (1½)"

7"

9½ (10½)"

2¾ (3½)"

4¾ (5½)"

4 (4½)"

SLEEVE

8 (8½)"

1½"

4¾ (6¼)"

6 (6¼)"

and, AT THE SAME TIME, after 3rd row of 2nd stripe (work measures 1½"/3.5cm from start of striped garter st), form buttonholes as follows:

Next row Work 3 sts in pat, yo, k2tog, work 10 (12) sts in pat, k2tog, yo, work 3 sts in pat, work to end. Rep this buttonhole row after the 5th and 8th stripes, and, AT THE SAME TIME, when front measures 11¾ (13½)"/30 (34)cm from cast-on edge, shape the armhole by binding off 8 sts at beg of next WS row—31 (36) sts. Cont straight until front measures 14½ (16)"/37 (41)cm from cast-on edge, at completion of 9th garter st stripe, then shape neck as follows:

Next row With RS facing, bind off 20 (22) sts, work to end—11 (14) sts. Cont straight until front measures 15½ (17¾)"/40 (45)cm from cast-on edge. Bind off remaining sts loosely for shoulder.

SLEEVES

Using size 2 (2.75mm) needles, cast on 40 (44) sts and work in garter st for 4 rows.

Next row Switch to size 3 (3.25mm) needles and St st, and inc 1 st at each end of row every 4 rows 5 (2) times, then again every 6 rows 2 (6) times—54 (60) sts. Cont straight until sleeve measures 5 (6¼)"/13 (16)cm from cast-on edge. Bind off loosely.

FINISHING

Sew the shoulder seams. Fit a sleeve into each armhole, and sew the sleeve and side seams. Overlap the 2 sides of the bib and slip stitch together along the bottom edge.
Back border: Using size 2 (2.75mm) needles, beg at left inner leg with RS facing, pick up and knit 84 (104) sts around the crotch. Work in garter st for 3 rows, followed by St st for 4 rows. Bind off loosely.
Front border: Pick up as for left, beg at right inner leg with RS facing, and work in garter st for 3 rows.

Next row Switch to St st and form 7 buttonholes as follows: k 2 (3), yo, k2tog, *k 11 (14), yo, k2tog *, rep from * to *, knit to end. Complete band with 3 more rows in St st. Bind off.
Sew 6 buttons to the left front, opposite the buttonholes, and another 7 buttons to the back border of the crotch.

Cozy crib blanket

I'll stay warm and snuggly with my very own blankie.

SIZE

Approximately
24 x 26½ in/60 x 67cm

MATERIALS

❊ *4 5oz/140g skeins (each approx 153yd/140m) of Lion Brand Yarn Wool-Ease (acrylic/wool) in #620-099 Fisherman (Ecru)* ⑤

❊ *1 pair each size 6 (4mm) and 7 (4.5mm) needles*

STITCHES USED

❊ *stockinette stitch*
❊ *k1, p1 rib*
❊ *garter stitch*
❊ *moss stitch*

GAUGE

❊ *18 sts and 23 rows to 4"/10cm over moss st using size 7 (4.5mm) needles.*
Take time to check gauge.

CENTER

Work the central section in a single piece. Using size 7 (4.5mm) needles, cast on 105 sts and work 42 rows as follows: 35 sts in moss st, 35 sts alternating 6 rows k1, p1 rib and 6 rows St st, 35 sts moss st.

Now cont for another 42 rows, reversing the order of the patterns. Complete the center by repeating the first 42 rows. Do not cut the yarn.

BORDER

Switch to size 6 (4mm) needles and work *4 rows garter st **, 2 rows St st *, rep from * to * then from * to ** and, AT THE SAME TIME, inc at each end of every 4th row 3 times. Using size 6 (4mm) needles, with RS facing, pick up and knit 75 sts along another side of the blanket and repeat the border. Repeat for the remaining 2 sides. Slip stitch the diagonal seams at the corners.

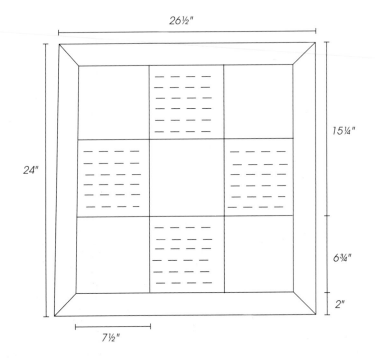

His and hers

A sweet pink wrap-front cardi or a charming blue pullover . . .
I can't decide which one I like best!

WRAP-FRONT CARDIGAN

SIZES
Newborn (3 months)

MATERIALS
❋ *2 (2) 1¾oz/50g skeins
(each approx 196yd/
180m) of Bergère de
France Caline (acrylic/
wool/polyamide) in
Porcinet (Pink)*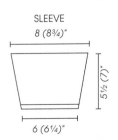
❋ *1 pair each
size 2 (2.75mm) and
3 (3.25mm) needles*
❋ *Three ½"/12mm
pink buttons*
❋ *One press stud*

STITCHES USED
❋ *stockinette stitch*
❋ *garter stitch*

GAUGE
❋ *27 sts and 36 rows to
4"/10cm over St st using
size 3 (3.25mm) needles.
Take time to check gauge.*

BACK
Using size 2 (2.75mm) needles, cast on 60 (66) sts and work in garter st for 6 rows.
Next row Switch to size 3 (3.25mm) needles and work straight in St st until back measures 4¼ (4¾)"/11 (12)cm from cast-on edge, then shape armholes as follows:
Cast off 6 sts at beg of next 2 rows, then cont straight until back measures 8¼ (9)"/21 (23) cm from cast-on edge. Bind off.

RIGHT FRONT
Using size 2 (2.75mm) needles, cast on 43 (47) sts and work in garter st for 6 rows.
Next row Switch to size 3 (3.25mm) needles and St st, working straight until right front measures 4¼ (4¾)"/11 (12)cm from cast-on edge, then shape neckline and armhole as follows:
Next row With RS facing, bind off 4 sts, knit to end. **Next row** Bind off 6 sts, purl to end.
Next row Bind off 3 sts, knit to end. Work 1 row straight.
Next row K2, sl 2 sts knitwise, k1, then pass the 2 slipped sts over the knitted st. Work 1 row straight. Rep the last 2 rows 4 (5) times. Work 2 rows straight.

Next row K2, SKP, knit to end. Work 3 rows straight. Rep the last 4 rows 1 (2) times—11 sts. Cont straight until right front measures 8¼ (9)"/21 (23)cm from cast-on edge, ending with a RS row. Bind off. Cast on and work left front as for right, reversing the shaping.

SLEEVES
Using size 2 (2.75mm) needles, cast on 42 (44) sts and work in garter st for 6 rows.
Next row Switch to size 3 (3.25mm) needles and St st. Cont straight for 5 rows, then shape sleeve as follows:
Next row K2, inc 1, work until 2 sts remain, inc 1, k2. Rep this inc row every 6 rows 3 (4) times, then every 8 rows 2 (3) times—54 (60) sts. Cont straight until sleeve measures 5½ (7)"/14 (18)cm from cast-on edge. Bind off.

BORDERS
For neck border, using size 3 (3.25mm) needles, cast on 150 (160) sts and work in St st for 6 rows. Bind off loosely. Cast on 55 (60) sts and complete the border in the same manner.

FINISHING
Sew the shoulder seams. Insert a sleeve in each armhole and sew up the sleeve and side seams. Beg at right front, sew the larger border around the neck, leaving the excess free. Sew the end of the smaller border under the right sleeve. Attach 3 buttons down the left neckline (see photo) and attach the press stud at the V of the neckline.

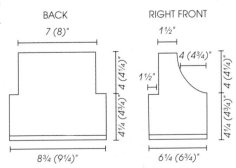

SLEEVE
8 (8¾)"

5½ (7)"

6 (6¼)"

BACK
7 (8)"

8¾ (9¼)"

RIGHT FRONT
1½"

4 (4¾)"

1½"

6¼ (6¾)"

4¼ (4¾)" 4 (4¼)"

4¼ (4¾)" 4 (4¼)"

PULLOVER

SIZES

Newborn (3 months)

MATERIALS

❈ *2 (2) 1¾ oz/50g skeins (each approx 196yd/180m) of Bergère de France Caline (acrylic/wool/polyamide) in Flipper (Light Blue)* 🔲1

❈ *1 pair each size 2 (2.75mm) and 3 (3.25mm) needles*

❈ *Six ½"/12mm blue buttons*

STITCHES USED

❈ *stockinette stitch*

❈ *p2, k1 rib*

❈ *single dec (SKP)*

GAUGE

❈ *27 sts and 36 rows to 4"/10cm over St st using size 3 (3.25mm) needles. Take time to check gauge.*

BACK

Using size 2 (2.75mm) needles, cast on 62 (65) sts and work in p2, k1 rib until back measures ¾"/2cm from cast-on edge.

Next row Switch to size 3 (3.25mm) needles and St st, increasing 3 times evenly over the course of the row—65 (68) sts. Cont straight until back measures 4¾ (5½)"/12 (14)cm from cast-on edge, then shape raglan armholes as follows:

Bind off 3 (2) sts at beg of next 2 rows.

Next row K2, k2tog, knit until 4 sts remain, SKP, k2. Rep this dec row every 2 rows 18 (20) times until 19 (22) sts remain and back measures 9 (10¼)"/23 (26)cm from cast-on edge. Bind off.

FRONT

Using size 2 (2.75mm) needles, cast on 62 (65) sts and work in p2, k1 rib until front measures ¾"/2cm from cast-on edge.

Next row Switch to size 3 (3.25mm) needles and St st, increasing 1 (3) sts evenly over the course of the row—63 (68) sts. Cont straight until front measures 4¾ (5½)"/12 (14)cm from cast-on edge, then shape raglan armholes as follows:

Bind off 3 (2) sts at beg of next 2 rows.

Next row K2, k2tog, knit until 4 sts remain, SKP, k2. Rep this dec row every 2 rows 15 (17) times

and, AT THE SAME TIME, when front measures 7 (8)"/18 (20)cm from cast-on edge, bind off the central 9 (10) sts for the neck and place the sts just worked on a holder while you complete the 2 sides separately. Continue to dec at raglan edge and, AT THE SAME TIME, dec by binding off at neck edge (RS rows) as follows: 3 sts once, 2 sts once, 1 st 1 (2) times, until 2 sts remain. Work 1 row straight and bind off. With WS facing, pick up the sts from the holder and complete the other side, reversing the neck shaping.

RIGHT SLEEVE

Using size 2 (2.75mm) needles, cast on 44 (47) sts and work in p2, k1 rib until sleeve measures ½"/1.5cm from cast-on edge.

Next row Switch to size 3 (3.25mm) needles and St st, increasing 5 times evenly over the course of the row—49 (52) sts. Cont straight in St st for 5 rows.

Next row K2, inc 1, work until 2 sts remain, inc 1, k2. Rep this inc row every 6 rows once, then every 8 rows 2 (3) times—57 (62) sts. Cont straight until sleeve measures 4¼ (5½)"/11 (14)cm from cast-on edge, then shape raglan seam as follows:

Bind off 3 (2) sts at beg of next 2 rows.

Next row K2, k2tog, knit until 4 sts remain, SKP, k2. Rep this dec row every 2 rows 15 (17) times more.

Next row Cont to dec at end of row another 3 times, and, AT THE SAME TIME, for smaller size bind off 4 sts at beg of next RS row 4 times (for larger size bind off 5 sts at beg of next RS row 3 times and 4 sts at beg of foll RS row once). Cast on and work the left sleeve in the same manner, reversing the shaping.

FINISHING

Using size 2 (2.75mm) needles, beg at right front with RS facing, pick up and knit 30 (36) sts across the neck and work in p2, k1 rib for 6 rows, beg row 1 with k2, then alternating

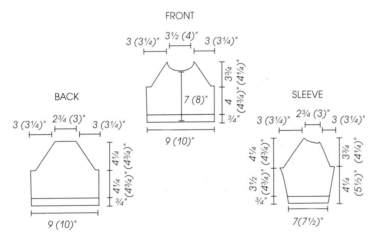

FRONT

3 (3¼)" 3½ (4)" 3 (3¼)"

7 (8)"

3¾ (4¾) (4¼)"

4 (4¾) (4¼)"

¾"

9 (10)"

BACK

3 (3¼)" 2¾ (3)" 3 (3¼)"

4¼ (4¾) (4¼)"

4¼ (4¾) (4¼)"

¾"

9 (10)"

SLEEVE

3 (3¼)" 2¾ (3)" 3 (3¼)"

4¼ (4¾) (4¼)"

3½ (4¾) (4¼)"

¾"

3¾ (4¼)"

4¼ (5½)"

7 (7½)"

p2, k1, and end with p2. Bind off loosely in rib. Using the same needles, with RS facing, pick up and knit 36 (39) sts down the right front raglan seam and work in p2, k1 rib as for the neck for 6 rows, forming buttonholes in row 3, beg at neck edge, as follows: work 3 sts in rib, yo, k2tog, *work 12 (13) sts in rib, yo, k2tog *, rep from * to * once, work in rib to end.

Repeat for left, beg at lower edge of raglan seam.

Sew up the raglan seams for the back and the sleeves. Using size 2 (2.75mm) needles, beg at top right sleeve with RS facing, pick up and knit 48 (54) sts across the sleeves and the back neck. Beg with k2, work in p2, k1 rib for 6 rows, alternating p2, k1, and end with k2. Bind off. Sew the side seams, then the sleeve seams, and the bottoms of the raglan seams. Sew the front button bands, and then sew the buttons opposite the buttonholes.

Ribbed jacket

So simple and stylish, I'd like one in every color.

SIZES

Newborn (3 months)

MATERIALS

* 6 (8) 1¾ oz/50g skeins
  (each approx
  98yd/90m) of Lion Brand
  Yarn Baby Wool (total
  easy-care wool) in
  #823-144 Lavender (4)
* 1 pair size 7 (4.5mm)
  needles
* Two ½"/12mm white
  buttons

STITCH USED

* fisherman's rib
  (see p. 10)

GAUGE

* 17 sts and 36 rows to
  4"/10cm over
  fisherman's rib using size
  7 (4.5mm) needles.
  Take time to check gauge.

BODY

Work the body section in a single piece using a double strand of yarn.

Cast on 93 (105) sts and work in fisherman's rib until body measures 4¼ (5)"/11 (13)cm from cast-on edge.

Next row Work 25 (29) sts in rib pat for the left back and place these sts on a stitch holder; continue the 2 sides separately from this point beg with right front. Bind off the next 7 sts for the left armhole, work 29 (33) sts in rib pat for the front and place these sts on a stitch holder; bind off the foll 7 sts for the right armhole and cont in rib over the remaining 25 (29) sts until right back measures 8¼ (9½)"/21 (24)cm from cast-on edge. Bind off loosely.

Work across the 25 (29) sts from the first holder and complete the left back to match the right.

Now work across the remaining 29 (33) sts and cont in fisherman's rib until front measures 7 (8¼)"/18 (21)cm from cast-on edge, then shape the neck as follows:

Next row Work 9 (10) sts in rib pat and place these sts on a stitch holder; complete the 2 sides of the front separately from this point, beg with right. Bind off the next 11 (13) sts for the neck and work 9 (10) sts in rib. Cont in rib until right front measures 8¼ (9½)"/21 (24)cm from cast-on edge. Bind off loosely. Work across the sts on the holder and complete the left front to match the right.

SLEEVES

Using a double strand of yarn, cast on 27 (31) sts and work in fisherman's rib until sleeve measures 3"/8cm from cast-on edge.

Next row K1, inc 1, work in rib pat until 1 st remains, inc 1, k1. Rep this inc row every 10 (12) rows twice more, incorporating the inc sts into the ribbing—33 (37) sts. Cont straight until sleeve measures 7½ (8¼)"/19 (21)cm from cast-on edge. Bind off loosely.

FINISHING

Sew the shoulder seams. Sew a sleeve into each armhole and sew up the sleeve seams, working the first 1½"/4cm of the seam on the outside to allow for a turned-back cuff. Using a tapestry needle or crochet hook, work a buttonhole loop at the corner of the left back and on the straight edge of the neck, as shown in the photo. Sew the buttons on the right back.

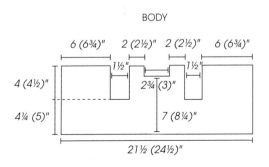

BODY

6 (6¾)" 2 (2½)" 2 (2½)" 6 (6¾)"

1½" 1½"

4 (4½)"

2¾ (3)"

4¼ (5)"

7 (8¼)"

21½ (24½)"

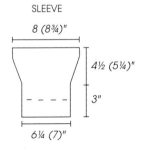

SLEEVE

8 (8¾)"

4½ (5¼)"

3"

6¼ (7)"

※ The jacket is
photographed from
the back to show
the buttons.

Warm and cozy

Long johns and booties have never been so elegant!

LONG JOHNS

SIZES

Newborn (3 months)

MATERIALS

❋ 2 (3) 1¾oz/50g skeins (each approx 196yd/ 180m) of Bergère de France Caline (acrylic/ wool/polyamide) in Nono (Gray) ❶

❋ 1 pair each sizes 2 (2.75mm) and 3 (3.25mm) needles

❋ Cable needle

❋ Nine ½"/12mm gray buttons

❋ White elastic thread

STITCHES USED

❋ stockinette stitch

❋ garter stitch

❋ p2, k1 rib

❋ cable pattern (follow the chart on p. 31)

❋ single dec (SKP)

GAUGE

❋ 30 sts and 36 rows to 4"/10cm over cable pattern using size 3 (3.25mm) needles.

Take time to check gauge.

BACK

Beg with the left leg. Using size 2 (2.75mm) needles, cast on 32 sts and work in p2, k1 rib until leg measures 2"/5cm from cast-on edge.

Next row Switch to size 3 (3.25mm) needles and cable pat, and work straight until leg measures 3¾ (4¼)"/9 (11)cm from cast-on edge. Leave these sts on a stitch holder. For the right leg, cast on and work as given for the left. After completing last row, cast on 13 (22) sts for the crotch, working the new sts into the cable pattern, and cont across the left leg sts—77 (86) sts.

Cont straight until back measures 10½ (12½)"/27 (32)cm from cast-on edge.

**Next row For the yoke, switch to size 2 (2.75mm) needles and p2, k1 rib. Work straight until back measures 11½ (13½)"/29 (34)cm from cast-on edge, then shape the armholes as follows:

Bind off 4 sts at beg of next 2 rows, 2 sts at beg of foll 4 rows, then 1 st at beg of next 4 rows—57 (66) sts. Cont straight until back measures 14½ (17)"/37 (43)cm from cast-on edge, then shape the neck as follows:

Work 16 (19) sts in rib pat and place these sts on a stitch holder; complete the 2 sides separately from this point, beg with left back. Bind off the next 25 (28) sts for the neck and work in rib pat to end. Work 1 row straight in rib pat.

Next row Bind off 5 sts (neck edge), work in rib to end—11 (14) sts. Cont in rib until left back measures 15 (17¼)"/38 (44)cm from cast-on edge. Bind off. Work across the sts on the holder and complete the right back, reversing the shaping.

FRONT

Cast on and work as given for back as far as **.

Next row For the yoke, switch to size 2 (2.75mm) needles and in p2, k1 rib work 30 (34) sts. Cast on 8 sts and turn the work. Leave the remaining 47 (52) sts on a stitch holder and complete the 2 sides separately from this point, continuing on the 38 (42) sts of the left front. Work straight until left front measures 11½ (13½)"/29 (34)cm from cast-on edge, then shape the armhole as follows: Bind off 4 sts at beg of next RS row, 2 sts at beg of foll RS row twice, and 1 st at beg of next RS row twice—28 (32) sts.

Cont straight until left front measures 13½ (15¾)"/34 (40)cm from cast-on edge, ending with a RS row. For neck, bind off at beg of WS rows as follows: 6 (7) sts, 5 sts, 3 sts, 2 sts, and 1 st—11 (14) sts. Cont straight until left front measures 15 (17¼)"/38 (44)cm from cast-on edge. Bind off. Work across the 47 (52) sts on the holder and cont in p2, k1 rib until right front measures 11½ (13½)"/29 (34)cm from cast-on edge, ending with a RS row. Bind off 4 sts at beg of next WS row, 2 sts at beg of foll WS row twice, and 1 st at beg of next WS row twice, and, AT THE SAME TIME, when right front measures 11¾ (14)"/30 (36)cm from cast-on edge, on next RS row work a buttonhole: work 3 sts in rib pat, yo, k2tog, work in rib to end. Rep this buttonhole row 1"/2.5cm higher. Cont straight until right front measures 13½ (15¾)"/34 (40) cm from cast-on edge, ending with a WS row. For neck, bind off at beg of RS rows as follows: 10 (12) sts, 5 sts, 4 sts twice, 2 sts, and

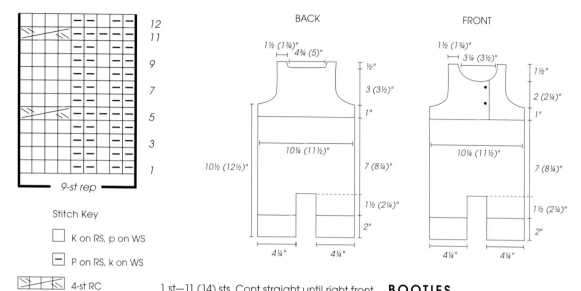

Stitch Key

☐ K on RS, p on WS

⊟ P on RS, k on WS

▧ 4-st RC

9-st rep

Chart rows: 1, 3, 5, 7, 9, 11, 12

BACK

1½ (1¾)"
4¾ (5)"
½"
3 (3½)"
1"
10¼ (11½)"
10½ (12½)"
7 (8¼)"
1½ (2¼)"
2"
4¼"   4¼"

FRONT

1½ (1¾)"
3¼ (3½)"
1½"
2 (2¼)"
1"
10¼ (11½)"
7 (8¼)"
1½ (2¼)"
2"
4¼"   4¼"

1 st—11 (14) sts. Cont straight until right front measures 15 (17¼)"/38 (44)cm from cast-on edge. Bind off.

FINISHING

Sew the shoulder seams. Using size 2 (2.75mm) needles, beg at right front with RS facing, pick up and knit 65 (73) sts around the neck. Work in St st for 4 rows, beg with a purl row. Bind off loosely. Using size 2 (2.75mm) needles and beg at left front underarm with RS facing, pick up and knit 60 (68) sts around the armhole. Work as for neck border and bind off loosely. Rep for right, beg at right back underarm.

Using size 2 (2.75mm) needles, beg at inside left leg with RS facing, pick up and knit 60 (66) sts around the back crotch and repeat the same border. Pick up and knit the same number of sts, beg at inside right leg of front, and purl 1 row, then work buttonholes as follows:

Next row K3 (4), yo, k2tog, *k 11 (12), yo, k2tog *, rep from * to * 3 times more, knit to end. Complete 2 more rows in St st and bind off loosely.

Sew the side seams and slip stitch the 8 sts at the back of the placket in place. Sew the buttons facing the buttonholes.

BOOTIES

Beg at the top of the ankle. Using size 2 (2.75mm) needles, cast on 38 (44) sts and work in St st for 4 rows.

Next row Switch to p2, k1 rib and work straight until bootie measures 1¼ (1¾)"/ 3 (4)cm from cast-on edge. Now place the first and last 13 (16) sts of the work on spare needles or stitch holders and cont over the central 12 sts for the upper, working in p2, k1 rib for another 1¾ (2)"/4 (5)cm. Cut the yarn and leave these sts on a spare needle. Work in rib pat across the first 13 (16) sts left aside, then pick up and knit 12 (15) sts along the edge of the upper, work in rib across the 12 central sts, pick up and knit 12 (15) sts along the other edge of the upper, work the remaining 13 (16) sts left aside in rib—62 (74) sts. Work in rib pat for 8 (10) rows, and cut the yarn. For the sole, place the first and last 25 (31) sts on spare needles and cont in garter st over the 12 central sts as follows: *k11, k2tog (k 1 st from the sole tog with 1 st from those left aside), turn the work, k11, sl 1, k1 (from sts left aside), psso, turn the work *, rep from * to * until 6 (8) sts remain on each side. Bind off. Sew up the back of the bootie and the sole. Attach a button at the front. Pass a length of elastic thread through the ribbing at the ankle. Complete another, identical bootie.

Rolled-sleeve tunic

A little go-with-everything tunic, so trendy with its rolled sleeves.

SIZES

3 (6) months

MATERIALS

❋ 2 (3) 1¾oz/50g skeins
   (each approx
   125yd/115m) of Bergère
   de France Sonora
   (acrylic/cotton) in Aloes
   (Pale Green) (4)
❋ 1 pair size 4 (3.5mm)
   needles
❋ Six ½"/12mm buttons

STITCHES USED

❋ stockinette stitch
❋ reverse stockinette stitch
❋ k2, p2 rib
❋ single dec (SKP)
❋ double dec (SK2P)

GAUGE

❋ 24 sts and 32 rows to
   4"/10cm over rev St st
   using size 4 (3.5mm)
   needles.
Take time to check gauge.

BODY

Work the body in a single section, beg at the front.

Cast on 62 (66) sts and work in k2, p2 rib until front measures 2"/5cm from cast-on edge.

Next row Switch to rev St st and dec 10 (8) times evenly over the course of the row—52 (58) sts.

Cont straight until body measures 3½ (4)"/9 (10)cm from cast-on edge. For the cap sleeves, cast on 6 sts at beg of next 2 rows—64 (70) sts. Cont straight until front measures 6¾ (7½)"/17 (19)cm from cast-on edge.

Next row To shape the neck, work 28 (29) sts and place on a stitch holder; bind off the next 8 (12) sts for the neck and cont on the 28 (29) sts for one side only. Work 1 row straight.

Next row *With RS facing, p2, SK2P, work to end *. Work 1 row straight.

Next row For 3-month size, **p2, SKP, work to end **; (for 6-month size, rep from * to *). Work 1 row straight. Both sizes: Rep from ** to ** every 2 rows twice (once)—23 sts.

Cont straight until front measures 8¼ (9)"/21 (23)cm from cast-on edge. For the right back, cast on 11 (13) sts—34 (36) sts. Work straight in rev St st for 2 rows.

Next row For buttonhole, k2, yo, k2tog, work to end. Rep this buttonhole row every 10 rows twice more. Work 1 row straight.

Next row With RS facing, bind off 2 sts and leave the remaining 32 (34) sts on a spare needle.

Work across the 28 (29) sts on the stitch holder and rep the dec rows to form the neck, reversing the shaping by working until either 5 or 4 sts remain, then working either k3tog or k2tog thus: 3 months: k3tog once, k2tog 3 times (6 months: k3tog twice, k2tog

twice). For the left back, cast on 11 (13) sts and cont as given for right back, omitting the buttonholes and binding off the final 2 sts at beg of a WS row.

Now work across all the sts and place them again on a single needle—64 (68) sts. Cont straight until body measures 13 (14)"/33 (36) cm from cast-on edge (end of sleeves). Bind off 6 sts at beg of next 2 rows—52 (56) sts. Cont straight until body measures 14½ (16)"/37 (41)cm from cast-on edge.

Next row Cont in rev St st, increasing 10 (8) times evenly over the course of the row—62 (64) sts.

Next row Switch to k2, p2 rib and cont straight until body measures 16½ (18)"/42 (46)cm from cast-on edge. Bind off.

SHOULDER TABS (MAKE 2)

Cast on 8 sts and work in St st until tab measures 3"/7cm from cast-on edge. Bind off.

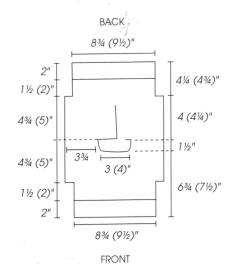

BACK

8¾ (9½)"

2"

1½ (2)"

4¼ (4¾)"

4¾ (5)"

4 (4¼)"

3¾

1½"

3 (4)"

4¾ (5)"

1½ (2)"

6¾ (7½)"

2"

8¾ (9½)"

FRONT

FINISHING

Beg at left back neck with RS facing, pick up and knit 52 (60) sts around the neck and work 2 rows in St st, beg with purl row. Bind off loosely. Sew the side and sleeve seams. Let the sleeve edges roll naturally, and hold the rolls in place with a few little stitches at the shoulder and underarm. Sew a tab under each roll and attach on top of the shoulder with a button. Sew a button at center front neck. Sew 2 buttons to the back opening, facing the buttonholes.

Cropped jacket

Lilac is the perfect complement to my rosy pink complexion.

SIZES

3 (6) months

MATERIALS

❊ 3 (3) 1¾oz/50g skeins
(each approx
103yd/95m) of Bergère
de France Bergereine
(wool/ cotton) in Baie
(Lilac) ③
❊ 1 pair size 4 (3.5mm)
needles
❊ Two ½"/12mm buttons
❊ Two press studs

STITCHES USED

❊ stockinette stitch
❊ fancy pattern stitch
(see chart)

GAUGE

❊ 26 sts and 36 rows to
4"/10cm over fancy
pattern st using size 4
(3.5mm) needles.
Take time to check gauge.

BODY

Complete the body in a single piece. Cast on 131 (145) sts and work 3 sts in St st (border), then follow the chart to work 131 (139) in fancy pattern stitch, ending with 3 sts in St st. Cont straight in pat as established until body measures 2¾ (3)"/7 (8)cm from cast-on edge.

Next row Work 37 (39) sts in pat for the right front, and place the remaining sts on a stitch holder for the moment. Cont straight in pat over 37 (39) sts until right front measures 5½ (6¼)"/14 (16)cm from cast-on edge. Bind off 16 sts at beg of next RS row for the neck—21 (23) sts. Cont in pat until right front measures 6¾ (7½)"/17 (19)cm from cast-on edge. Bind off. For the left front, work across the remaining 37 (39) sts and cont in fancy pat st until left front measures 5½ (6¼)"/14 (16)cm from cast-on edge. Bind off 16 sts at beg of next WS row for the neck—21 (23) sts. Cont in pat until left front measures 6¾ (7½)"/17 (19)cm from cast-on edge. Bind off.

SLEEVES

Cast on 39 (43) sts and work in fancy pat st for 3 rows.

Next row K1, inc 1, work in pat until 1 st remains, inc 1, k1. Rep this inc row, incorporating the new sts into the pattern, every 4 rows once, then every 6 rows 5 (7) times—53 (57) sts. Cont straight until sleeve measures 4¾ (5½)"/12 (14)cm from cast-on edge. Bind off.

FINISHING

Sew the shoulder seams. Fit a sleeve into each armhole and sew the side and sleeve seams. Sew 2 buttons on the right front, the first ¾"/2cm from the neck and the second 1¾"/4cm lower down. Sew the press studs to the right and left fronts under the buttons.

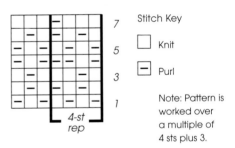

Stitch Key

☐ Knit

⊟ Purl

Note: Pattern is worked over a multiple of 4 sts plus 3.

4-st rep

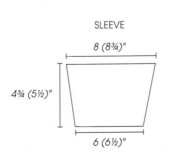

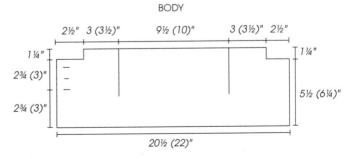

Pocketful of posies

I'll go flower picking in my rose-colored dress and matching booties.

DRESS

FRONT

Using size 3 (3.25mm) needles, cast on 62 (68) sts and work in garter st for 6 rows.

Next row Switch to size 4 (3.5mm) needles and St st. Work straight for 3 rows.

Next row K2, k2tog, knit until 4 sts remain, SKP, k2. Rep this dec row every 4 rows 3 times, then every 6 rows 3 (4) times—48 (52) sts. Cont straight until back measures 5 (6)"/13 (15)cm from cast-on edge. For the armholes, bind off 4 sts at beg of next row twice—40 (44) sts.

Next row Switch to k2, p2 rib, beg and end this row with k3 (instead of k2). Cont straight in k2, p2 rib until back measures 8 (9)"/20 (23)cm.

Next row Work 8 sts in rib pat and place these sts on a stitch holder; complete the 2 sides separately from this point. Bind off the next 24 (28) sts for the neck. Cont in rib on right front, working k3 (RS) at neck edge. Cont straight until right front measures 9 (10¼)"/23 (26)cm from cast-on edge. Bind off. Work across the 8 sts on the holder and complete the left front to match.

LEFT BACK

Using size 3 (3.25mm) needles, cast on 35 (40) sts and work in garter st for 6 rows.

Next row Switch to size 4 (3.5mm) needles and St st and work straight for 3 rows.

Next row Knit until 4 sts remain, SKP, k2. Rep this dec row every 4 rows 3 times, then every 6 rows 3 (4) times—28 (32) sts. Cont straight until left back measures 5 (6)"/13 (15)cm from cast-on edge. For armhole, bind off 4 sts at beg of next RS row—24 (28) sts, and switch to k2, p2 rib, working k3 at beg and end of the first RS rib row and, beg with first rib row, working 4 buttonholes as follows: k3, yo, k2tog, rib to end. Rep this buttonhole row every 10 (12) rows 3 times more. Cont straight until left back measures 9 (10¼)"/23 (26)cm from cast-on edge. Bind off.

Cast on and work the right front as for the left, reversing the shaping, working k2tog to dec in the skirt, and omitting the buttonholes.

SLEEVES

Using size 3 (3.25mm) needles, cast on 39 (44) sts and work in garter st for 6 rows.

Next row Switch to size 4 (3.5mm) needles and St st, increasing 5 times over the central sts in this first row—44 (49) sts. Work 4 rows straight.

Next row K2, inc 1, work until 2 sts remain, inc 1, k2. Rep this inc row every 6 rows once, then every 8 rows 2 (4) times—52 (57) sts. Cont straight until sleeve measures 5 (6)"/13 (15) cm from cast-on edge. Bind off.

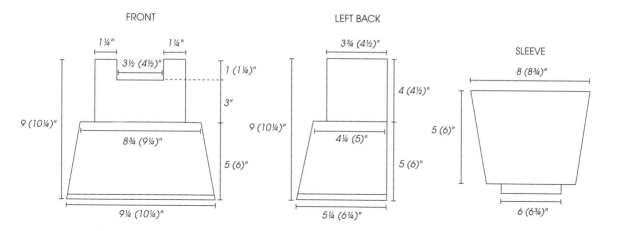

FRONT

1¼"   1¼"

3½ (4½)"

1 (1¼)"

3"

9 (10¼)"

8¾ (9¼)"

5 (6)"

9¼ (10¼)"

LEFT BACK

3¾ (4½)"

4 (4½)"

9 (10¼)"

4¼ (5)"

5 (6)"

5¼ (6¼)"

SLEEVE

8 (8¾)"

5 (6)"

6 (6¾)"

POCKETS (MAKE 2)

Using size 2 (2.75mm) needles, cast on 14 (16) sts and work in garter st for 20 (24) rows.
Next row K2tog, knit until 2 sts remain, k2tog. Rep this dec row every 2 rows 5 (6) times—2 sts. Bind off.

FINISHING

Sew the shoulder seams. Insert a sleeve in each armhole and sew the side and sleeve seams. Fold the flap of each pocket to the outside, and attach a flower button at the center. Slip stitch the pockets to the front, ¾"/2cm above the garter st border and 18 sts apart. Sew the 4 buttons to the right back, facing the buttonholes.

BOOTIES

Beg at center sole.
Using size 3 (3.25mm) needles, cast on 26 (28) sts and work in garter st for 1 row. Beg with next row, cont in garter st and dec 1 st at each end of every other row 5 times. Next, for the heel, cast on 5 (6) sts at beg of row, then inc 1 st at beg of every WS row 5 times to form the upper—26 (29) sts (10 rows for the upper).

Next row (row 11 of heel) Bind off 14 (15) sts—12 (14) sts. Cont straight in garter st for 8 rows.
Next row Cast on 14 (15) sts for the heel and cont decreasing 1 st at beg of every WS row 5 times—21 (24) sts at completion of row 10 of heel.
Next row With RS facing, bind off 5 (6) sts—16 (18) sts.
To complete the sole, cont increasing 1 st at each end of every other row 5 times—26 (28) sts. Bind off loosely.

FINISHING

Sew up the sole and heel seams. Sew the heel to the sole and sew up the toe. Attach the flower-shaped button at the front of the bootie, as shown in the photo.

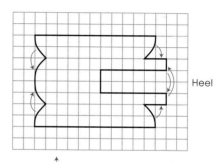

Heel

Direction of knitting

Dressed to the nines

I'm ready for a stroll around town in my classic ensemble.

CARDIGAN

SIZES
Newborn (3 months)

MATERIALS
✽ *3 (3) 1¾oz/50g balls*
   (each approx 137yd/
   125m) of Debbie Bliss/KFI
   Eco Baby (organic
   cotton) in #2 Grey **2**
✽ *1 pair size 2 (2.75mm)*
   needles
✽ *Two ½"/12mm light gray*
   buttons
✽ *Two press studs*

STITCHES USED
✽ *stockinette stitch*
✽ *seed stitch*
✽ *k1, p1 rib*
✽ *garter stitch*
✽ *single dec (SKP)*

GAUGE
✽ *28 sts and 40 rows to*
   4"/10cm over St st using
   size 2 (2.75mm) needles.
   Take time to check gauge.

40

BACK
Cast on 65 (71) sts and work in k1, p1 rib for 4 rows.
Next row Switch to St st and cont straight until back measures 2½ (3)"/6 (8)cm from cast-on edge, then shape the armholes as follows: Bind off 6 sts at beg of next 2 rows. Cont in St st until back measures 2¾ (3½)"/7 (9)cm from cast-on edge.
Next row Switch to seed st to complete the back. Cont straight until back measures 6 (7½)"/15 (19)cm from cast-on edge. Bind off loosely.

RIGHT FRONT
Cast on 37 (40) sts and work 4 rows as follows: 5 sts seed st, 32 (35) sts k1, p1 rib.
Next row Cont 5 sts seed st for the border and switch to St st for the remaining stitches. Cont straight until right front measures 2½ (3)"/6 (8)cm from cast-on edge, then shape the armholes. Bind off 6 sts at beg of next WS row. Cont as given until right front measures 2¾ (3½)"/7 (9)cm from cast-on edge.
Next row Switch to seed st to complete the

right front. Cont straight until right front measures 4¾ (6¼)"/12 (16)cm from cast-on edge, ending with a WS row, then shape the neck as follows:
Next row With RS facing, bind off 16 (17) sts—15 (17) sts. Cont straight until right front measures 5 (7½)"/15 (19)cm from cast-on edge, ending with a WS row. Bind off loosely. Left front: Work as for right, reversing the shaping.

SLEEVES
Cast on 39 (45) sts and work in k1, p1 rib for 4 rows.
Next row Switch to St st and work straight for 5 rows.
Next row K1, inc 1, work until 1 st remains, inc 1, k1. For smaller size rep this inc row every 6 rows twice, then every 8 rows 3 times (larger size: rep this inc row every 6 rows 7 times)—51 (61) sts. Cont straight until sleeve measures 5½ (6¼)"/14 (16)cm from cast-on edge. Bind off.

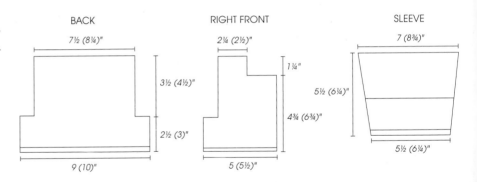

BACK
7½ (8¼)"
3½ (4½)"
2½ (3)"
9 (10)"

RIGHT FRONT
2¼ (2½)"
1¼"
4¾ (6¾)"
5 (5½)"

SLEEVE
7 (8¾)"
5½ (6¼)"
5½ (6¼)"

FINISHING
Make 4 bows as follows: Cast on 8 sts, work in garter st for 8 rows. Bind off. Form the bow shape by winding a strand of yarn several times around the middle of the band. Sew the shoulder seams. Insert a sleeve in each armhole and sew the sleeve and side seams. Sew the buttons to the borders and attach the buttons to the outside, the first ½"/1cm below the neck, the other 1¼"/3cm lower down. Attach a bow to each center front and to each sleeve at the last row of St st.

OVERALLS

BACK
Beg with left back leg. Using Navy, cast on 29 (33) sts and work in seed st for 6 rows.
Next row Switch to St st and work straight for 3 rows. Beg with next row, inc 1 st at beg of row (k2, inc 1) every 4 rows twice, then every 2 rows twice, and finally inc 2 (3) sts at beg and, AT THE SAME TIME, dec 1 st at the end of the row (work until 4 sts remain, SKP, k1) every 8 rows 8 times, then every 6 rows 4 times. Leave these sts on a spare needle. Cast on and work the right leg as for the left, reversing the shaping and working the dec as k2tog. After the last inc row, cast on 11 (13) sts for the crotch, work across the left leg sts from the spare needle, and cont in St st, decreasing at each side as before, until back measures 7¾ (9¼)"/19.5 (23.5)cm from crotch cast-on. Count off 27 sts at center back and place a contrasting marker on each side of them.
Next row Work in St st as far as marker, then work over the next 27 sts as follows: *p1, k2tog *, rep from * to * 3 times, p1, k1, p1, **k2tog, p1 **, rep from ** to ** 3 times, and cont in St st to end—55 (61) sts. Cont in pattern as established, knitting the knit sts and purling the purl sts on central sts in k1, p1 rib, for ¾"/2cm, then cont in St st over all sts to complete the back. Cont as given until back measures 8½ (10)"/21.5 (25.5)cm from cast-on edge.

SIZES
Newborn (3 months)

MATERIALS
❉ 3 (3) 1¾oz/50g balls (each approx 137yd/ 125m) of Debbie Bliss/KFI Eco Baby (organic cotton) #3 Navy (2)
❉ 2 (2) balls in #2 Grey
❉ 1 pair size 2 (2.75mm) needles
❉ Size B/1 (2.25mm) crochet hook
❉ Four ½"/12mm light-gray buttons
❉ Seven press studs
❉ Elastic thread

STITCHES USED
❉ stockinette stitch
❉ k1, p1 rib
❉ garter stitch
❉ seed stitch
❉ single dec (SKP)
❉ double dec (SK2P)

GAUGE
❉ 28 sts and 40 rows to 4"/10cm over St st using size 2 (2.75mm) needles.
Take time to check gauge.

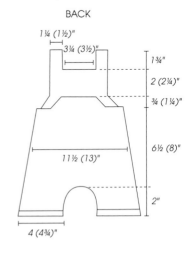

BACK

1¼ (1½)"
3¼ (3½)"
1¾"
2 (2¼)"
¾ (1¼)"
11½ (13)"
6½ (8)"
2"
4 (4¾)"

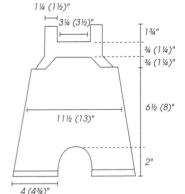

FRONT

1¼ (1½)"
3¼ (3½)"
1¾"
¾ (1¼)"
¾ (1¼)"
11½ (13)"
6½ (8)"
2"
4 (4¾)"

To shape the armholes, bind off 4 sts at beg of next 2 rows. Beg with next row, work the first 5 and the last 5 sts of each row in seed st, forming borders, and shape the yoke as follows: with RS facing, work 5 sts in pat, k2tog, work until 7 sts remain, SKP, work 5 sts in pat. Rep this dec row for smaller size every 2 rows 3 times (for larger size, every 2 rows and 4 rows alternately 3 times). After completing last dec row, work in seed st over all sts—39 (45) sts. Cont straight until back measures 11¼ (13½)"/28.5 (34.5)cm from cast-on edge.
Next row *Work 8 (10) sts in pat and place on a stitch holder. Complete the 2 sides separately from this point. Bind off the next 23 (25) sts for the neck and work in pattern to end. Cont in seed st over 8 (10) sts until shoulder strap measures 1¾"/4cm. Bind off. Pick up the sts from the holder and complete the other strap *.

FRONT

Cast on and work as for back until front measures 10 (12¼)"/25.5 (31.5)cm, then shape the neck by repeating from * to * as for back.

BOW

Cast on 8 sts, work in garter st for 8 rows. Bind off. Form the bow shape by winding a strand of yarn several times around the middle of the band.

FINISHING

Using Navy, beg at right front inside leg with RS facing, pick up and knit 36 (39) sts around the crotch. Work in St st for 6 rows. Bind off. Repeat for back, beg at left back inside leg with RS facing.
Pass the elastic thread through the k1, p1 ribbing on the WS to make gathers. Sew up the side seams. Sew the buttons on the front straps.
Sew a press stud to each strap, and another 5 press studs around the crotch. Attach the bow to center front above the gathers.

HAT

Using Grey, cast on 95 (107) sts and work in k1, p1 rib for 4 rows.
Next row Switch to seed st and work straight until hat measures 2½ (3)"/6.5 (7.5)cm from cast-on edge.
Next row Work 6 (7) sts in seed st pat, *SK2P, work 13 (15) sts in pat *, rep from * to * 4 times more, sl 1, k2tog, work 6 (7) sts in pat. Rep this dec row every 4 rows 5 (6) times more, working 1 less st after each dec with each dec row. After last dec row, work 2 rows straight.
Next row *K1, SK2P, k1 *, rep from * to * 6 times more—9 sts. Bind off.
Following the directions for the overalls, complete 1 bow in Navy and another in Grey. Using the crochet hook and Navy, work ch sts for one length of 1¼"/3cm and another length of 2½"/6cm.
Sew up the hat seam. Attach a bow to the end of each chain-st cord, and sew the cords to the top of the hat.

43

Pretty as a picture

A lovely dress for a lovely girl, with matching ballerina booties!

DRESS

SIZES
Newborn (3 months)

MATERIALS
❊ 3 (3) 1¾oz/50g balls (each approx 137yd/ 125m) of Debbie Bliss/KFI Eco Baby (organic cotton) #21 Plum 🔵2
❊ 2 (2) balls in #24 Apricot
❊ 1 pair size 2 (2.75mm) needles
❊ Four ½"/12mm light-gray buttons
❊ Four press studs
❊ Elastic thread

STITCHES USED
❊ stockinette stitch
❊ k1, p1 rib
❊ garter stitch
❊ seed stitch
❊ single dec (SKP)
❊ double dec (SK2P)

GAUGE
❊ 28 sts and 40 rows to 4"/10cm over St st using size 2 (2.75mm) needles.
Take time to check gauge.

BACK
Using Plum, cast on 81 (93) sts and work in seed st for 6 rows.
Next row Switch to St st. Cont straight for 7 rows.
Next row K2, k2tog, work until 4 sts remain, SKP, k2. Rep this dec row for smaller size every 8 rows 8 times (for larger size every 8 rows 7 times, then every 6 rows 4 times), and cont until back measures 7¾ (9¼)"/19.5 (23.5)cm from cast-on edge. Count off 27 sts at center back and place a contrasting marker on each side of them.
Next row Work in St st as far as marker, then work over the next 27 sts as follows: *p1, k2tog *, rep from * to * 3 times, p1, k1, p1, ** k2tog, p1 **, rep from ** to ** 3 times, and cont in St st to end—55 (61) sts. Cont in pattern as established, knitting the knit sts and purling the purl sts on central sts in k1, p1 rib for ¾"/2cm, then cont in St st over all sts to complete the back. Cont as given until back measures 8½ (10)"/21.5 (25.5)cm from cast-on edge.
To shape the armholes, bind off 4 sts at beg of next 2 rows. Beg with next row, work the first 5 and the last 5 sts of each row in seed st, forming borders, and shape the yoke as follows:
With RS facing, work 5 sts in seed st, k2tog, work until 7 sts remain, SKP, work 5 sts in seed st pat. Rep this dec row for smaller size every 2 rows 3 times (for larger size, every 2 rows and 4 rows alternately 3 times). After completing last dec row, work in seed st over

all sts—39 (45) sts. Cont straight until back measures 11¼ (13½)"/28.5 (34.5)cm from cast-on edge.
Next row *Work 8 (10) sts in seed st pat and place on a stitch holder. Complete the 2 sides separately from this point. Bind off the next 23 (25) sts for the neck and pattern to end. Cont in seed st over 8 (10) sts until shoulder strap measures 1¾"/4cm. Bind off. Pick up the sts from the holder and complete the other strap *.

FRONT
Cast on and work as for back until front measures 10 (12¼)"/25.5 (31.5)cm, then shape the neck by repeating from * to * as for back.

FINISHING
Using Apricot, make a bow as follows: Cast on 8 sts, work in garter st for 8 rows. Bind off. Form the bow shape by winding a strand of yarn several times around the middle of the band. Sew up the side seams. Pass the elastic thread through the k1, p1 ribbing on the WS to make gathers. Sew the buttons onto the front straps. Sew a press stud to each strap. Attach the bow to center front above the gathers.

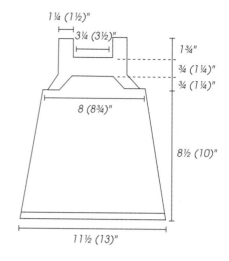

BACK

1¼ (1½)"

3¼ (3½)"

1¾"

2 (2¼)"

¾ (1¼)"

8 (8¾)"

8½ (10)"

11½ (13)"

FRONT

1¼ (1½)"

3¼ (3½)"

1¾"

¾ (1¼)"

¾ (1¼)"

8 (8¾)"

8½ (10)"

11½ (13)"

BALLET SLIPPERS

Using Apricot, cast on 29 (33) sts and work in garter st, increasing 4 times over the course of row 1 as follows: k2, inc, 1, k 12 (14), inc 1, k1, inc 1, k 12 (14), inc 1, k2. Rep this inc row every 2 rows twice more, working the inc on each side of the block of 12 (14) sts—45 (49) sts.

Next row Switch to seed st and cont for 8 rows straight.

Next row Dec as follows: work 17 (19) sts in pat, SK2P, work 5 sts in pat, k3tog, work 17 (19) sts in pat. Rep these dec on next row but one as follows: work 16 (18) sts in pat, SK2P, work 3 sts in pat, k3tog, work 16 (18) sts in pat.

Next row Bind off loosely. For each strap, using Apricot, cast on 8 sts and work in garter st for 6 rows. Bind off.

Sew a strap to one side of the bootie, then sew the button and a press stud to the other end. Complete a second bootie, reversing the placement of the strap.

Little man on campus

A snug jacket just like the ones the big kids wear.

SIZES

Newborn (3 months)

MATERIALS

❋ 2 (2) 1¾oz/50g skeins
   (each approx 87yd/80m)
   of Bergère de France
   Magic+ (superwash
   wool/acrylic) in
   Coral (A)
❋ 1 (1) skein each in
   Brebis (Light Gray) and
   Fonte (Dark Gray)
❋ 1 pair each
   size 7 (4.5mm) and
   9 (5.5mm) needles
❋ Five ½"(12mm) buttons

STITCHES USED

❋ stockinette stitch
❋ k2, p2 rib

GAUGE

❋ 18 sts and 22 rows to
   4"/10cm over St st using
   size 9 (5.5mm) needles.
   Take time to check gauge.

48

BACK

Using size 7 (4.5mm) needles and Dark Gray, cast on 48 (52) sts and work in k2, p2 rib, beg and end first row with k3. Cont straight until back measures 1¼"/3cm from cast-on edge.
Next row Switch to size 9 (5.5mm) needles and Coral, and work in St st, decreasing 7 (8) sts evenly over the course of the row—40 (45) sts. Cont straight until back measures 5½ (6¼)"/14 (16)cm from cast-on edge, then shape armholes as follows:
Bind off 3 sts at beg of next 2 rows—34 (39) sts. Cont straight until back measures 10 (11)"/25 (28)cm from cast-on edge. Bind off loosely.

RIGHT FRONT

Using size 7 (4.5mm) needles and Dark Gray, cast on 24 (26) sts and work in k2, p2 rib, beg and end first row with k3. Cont straight until back measures 1¼"/3cm from cast-on edge.
Next row Switch to size 9 (5.5mm) needles and Coral, and work in St st, decreasing 4 (5) sts evenly over the course of the row—20 (21) sts. Cont straight until back measures 5½ (6¼)"/14 (16)cm from cast-on edge, ending with a RS row, then shape armhole as follows.
Next row With WS facing, bind off 3 sts and work to end. Cont straight until right front measures 8¼ (9½)"/21 (24)cm from cast-on edge, ending with a WS row, then shape neck as follows:
Next row With RS facing, bind off 4 (6) sts, work to end. Work 1 row straight.
Next row K1, k3tog, work to end. Work 1 row straight.
***Next row** K1, k2tog, work to end. Work 1 row straight *. Rep from * to * 8 (9) sts. Cont straight until right front measures 10 (11)"/25 (28)cm from cast-on edge, ending with a RS row.

Next row Bind off loosely. For left front, cast on and work as for right, reversing the shaping.

SLEEVES

Using size 7 (4.5mm) needles and Dark Gray, cast on 26 (30) sts and work in k2, p2 rib until sleeve measures 1¼"/3cm from cast-on edge.
Next row Switch to size 9 (5.5mm) needles and Coral, and work in the foll stripes pattern: 4 rows Coral, 2 rows Dark Gray, 2 rows Coral, 2 rows Dark Gray, 4 rows Coral, 10 rows Light Gray, then cont in Coral to the end of the sleeve, and, AT THE SAME TIME, shape sleeve as follows: Work straight in St st for 3 rows.
Next row K1, inc 1, work until 1 st remains, inc 1, k1. Rep this inc row every 4 rows 6 (3) times (then, for larger size only, every 6 rows 3 times)—40 (44) sts. Cont straight until sleeve measures 6¼ (7)"/16 (18)cm from cast-on edge. Bind off loosely.

FINISHING

Sew up the shoulder seams. Using size 7 (4.5mm) needles and Dark Gray, beg at right front neck with RS facing, pick up and knit 48 (56) sts around the neck. Work in k2, p2 rib, beg and end first row with k3. Cont until neck border measures 1"/2.5cm from pick-up row. Bind off in rib pat. Using size 7 (4.5mm) needles and Gray, beg at left neck border with RS facing, pick up and knit 56 (64) sts down left front, beg and end first row with k3. Cont in rib until border measures 1"/2.5cm. Bind off in rib pat. Rep pick-up on right front, beg at lower right edge with RS facing, and work 1 row straight in rib.

Next row Work buttonholes as follows: work 3 sts in rib pat, yo, k2tog, *work 10 (12) sts in rib, yo, k2tog *, rep from * to * 3 times, work in rib to end. Cont in k2, p2 rib until border measures 1"/2.5cm. Bind off in rib. False pockets: Using size 7 (4.5mm) needles and Light Gray, cast on 16 sts and work in k2, p2 rib, beg and end first row with k3. Cont straight until false pocket measures 2"/5cm from cast-on edge. Bind off in rib. Fit a sleeve into each armhole and sew up the sleeve seams and side seams. Slip stitch the false pockets 1¾"/4cm from the ribbing, and 1"/2.5cm from the front borders. Attach the buttons to the left front, opposite the buttonholes.

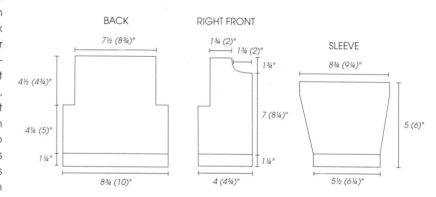

BACK

7½ (8¾)"

4½ (4¾)"

4¼ (5)"

1¼"

8¾ (10)"

RIGHT FRONT

1¾ (2)"

1¾ (2)"

1¾"

7 (8¼)"

1¼"

4 (4¾)"

SLEEVE

8¾ (9¼)"

5 (6)"

5½ (6¼)"

Shades of gray

A subtly striped pullover and matching scarf, for a chic winter outfit.

PULLOVER

SIZES
Newborn (3 months)

MATERIALS
❋ 1 (1) 1¾oz/50g skein
   each (each approx
   138yd/126m) of
   Schoeller + Stahl/Skacel
   Collection Fortissima
   6-Ply (wool/nylon) in
   2248 Natural, 2254 Grey/
   White Twist, and 2256
   Grey Heather (1️⃣)
❋ 1 pair sizes 2 (2.75mm)
   and 3 (3.25mm) needles
❋ Two ½"/12mm buttons
❋ Two press studs

STITCHES USED
❋ k1, p1 rib
❋ stockinette stitch
❋ garter stitch

GAUGE
❋ 27 sts and 34 rows to
   4"/10cm over St st using
   size 3 (3.25mm) needles.
   Take time to check gauge.

BACK
* Using size 2 (2.75mm) needles and Grey Heather, cast on 67 (73) sts and work in k1, p1 rib until back measures ¾"/2cm from cast-on edge.
Next row Switch to size 3 (3.25mm) needles and St st, and dec 5 (6) times evenly across the row—62 (67) sts.
Cont straight until back measures 2¾ (3½)"/7 (9)cm. Beg with next row, cont with 2 rows Grey/White Twist, 2 rows Grey Heather, and cont with Grey/White Twist until back measures 4¼ (5)"/11 (13)cm from cast-on edge, then shape the armholes. Bind off 7 sts at beg of next 2 rows—48 (53) sts, then cont straight until back measures 5 (6)"/13 (15) cm from cast-on edge. Beg with next row, cont with 2 rows Natural, 2 rows Gray/White Twist, then cont with Natural to complete the back *. Work straight until back measures 7½ (9)"/19 (23)cm from cast-on edge, then shape the neck as follows.
Next row K 17 (18) and place these sts on a stitch holder; complete the 2 sides separately from this point. Bind off the next 14 (17) sts for the neck, knit to end. Work 1 row straight.
Next row Bind off 5 sts (neck edge), knit to end—12 (13) sts. Cont straight until left back measures 8 (9¼)"/20 (24)cm from cast-on edge, ending with a RS row. Bind off. Work across the sts on the holder and complete the right back, reversing the shaping.

FRONT
Cast on and work as for back from * to *. Work straight until front measures 6¼ (8)"/16 (20)cm from cast-on edge, then shape the neck as follows:
Next row K21 (22) and place these sts on a stitch holder; complete the 2 sides separately from this point. Bind off the next 6 (9) sts for the neck and knit to end. Work 1 row straight.
Next row Bind off 3 sts, knit to end. Work 1 row straight **.
Next row Bind off 2 sts, knit to end. Work 1 row straight **. Rep from ** to **.
Next row Bind off 2 sts, knit to end—12 (13) sts. Cont straight until right front measures 7½ (9)"/19 (23)cm from cast-on edge, ending with a RS row. Bind off. Work across the sts on the holder and complete the left front, reversing the shaping.

SLEEVES
Using size 2 (2.75mm) needles and Grey Heather, cast on 41 (47) sts and work in k1, p1 rib for ½"/1cm.
Next row Switch to size 3 (3.25mm) needles and St st and work the following stripes: ** 2 rows Grey Heather, 2 rows Grey/White Twist **, rep from ** to ** 5 times followed by * 2 rows Natural, 2 rows Grey/White Twist *, rep from * to * once, then cont in Natural to complete the sleeve while, AT THE SAME TIME, shaping the sleeve beg with row 8 (6) as follows: k1, inc 1, work until 1 st remains, inc 1, k1. Rep this inc row every 8 (6) rows 3 (2) times—49 (59) sts. Cont straight until sleeve measures 5½ (6¾)"/14 (17)cm from cast-on edge. Bind off loosely.

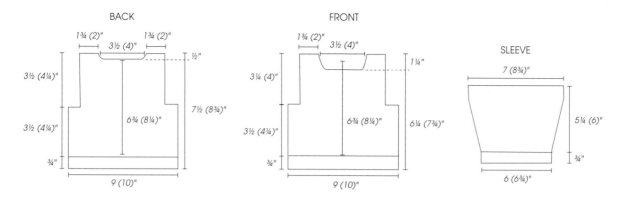

BACK

1¾ (2)" 1¾ (2)"
3½ (4)"
½"
3½ (4¼)"
3½ (4¼)"
6¾ (8¼)"
7½ (8¾)"
¾"
9 (10)"

FRONT

1¾ (2)"
3½ (4)"
1¼"
3¼ (4)"
3½ (4¼)"
6¾ (8¼)"
6¼ (7¾)"
¾"
9 (10)"

SLEEVE

7 (8¾)"
5¼ (6)"
¾"
6 (6¾)"

FINISHING

Using size 2 (2.75mm) needles and Natural, beg at right back shoulder edge, pick up and knit 54 (59) sts, ending at left back shoulder edge. Work in garter st for 4 rows. Bind off loosely.

Using size 2 (2.75mm) needles and Natural, beg at left front shoulder edge, pick up and knit 57 (62) sts, ending at right front shoulder edge. Work in garter st for 4 rows. Bind off loosely. Lap the front border over the back border and hold in place with a few slip stitches at the shoulder edge. Insert a sleeve into each armhole, and sew up the side and sleeve seams.

Sew a press stud to the border at each shoulder, and attach a button on top of each press stud.

SCARF

Using size 2 (2.75mm) needles and Grey Heather, cast on 21 (23) sts and work in k1, p1 rib for ½"/1cm.

Next row Switch to size 3 (3.25mm) needles and St st, working the following stripes: ° * 2 rows Grey Heather, 2 rows Grey/White Twist *, rep from * to * 5 times, ** 2 rows Natural, 2 rows Grey/White Twist **, rep from ** to ** once, now work 16 rows Natural, followed by *° 2 rows Grey/White Twist, 2 rows Natural *°, rep from *° to *° once, then °°work 2 rows Grey/White Twist, 2 rows Grey Heather °°, rep from °° to °° 5 times, now work 12 rows Grey Heather °, and rep from ° to ° twice. Finally, using Grey Heather, work in k1, p1 rib for ½"/1cm. Bind off in rib. Using Natural, make 2 pompoms 1¼"/3cm in diameter, and attach one to each end of the scarf.

POMPOM

Cut 2 cardboard circles as shown in the sketch. Place the circles together and wind several layers of yarn through the center hole. Cut the yarn between the cardboard circles. Before removing the circles, tie the yarn very tightly, leaving a length for attaching the pompom. Cut to the center of the cardboard and remove the circles.

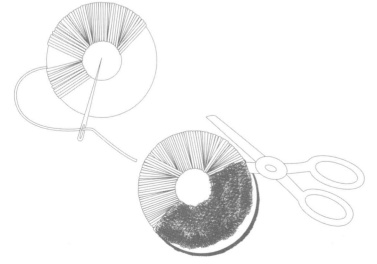

Just like grandpa

Soft as can be to keep me warm and happy.

SIZES

Newborn (3 months)

MATERIALS

❊ 2 (2) 1¾oz/50g skeins
   (each approx 137yd/
   125m) of Bergère de
   France Ideal (superwash
   wool/acrylic/polyamide)
   Marin (Dark Blue) **3**

❊ 1 pair each
   size 2 (2.75mm) and
   3 (3.25mm) needles

❊ Three ½"(12mm) buttons

❊ Two press studs

STITCHES USED

❊ k2, p2 rib

❊ fancy pattern stitch:
   2 rows stockinette stitch,
   4 rows garter stitch

GAUGE

❊ 28 sts and 48 rows to
   4"/10cm over fancy pat
   st using size 3 (3.25mm)
   needles.

Take time to check gauge.

BACK

Using size 2 (2.75mm) needles, cast on 74 (82) sts and work in k2, p2 rib for ¾"/2cm.

Next row Switch to size 3 (3.25mm) needles and fancy pat st, decreasing 12 (14) times evenly over the course of the row—62 (68) sts. Cont in pat st until back measures 4¼ (4¾)"/11 (12)cm from cast-on edge, then shape armholes as follows:

Bind off 6 sts at beg of next 2 rows—50 (56) sts. Cont straight in pat st until back measures 8 (8¾)"/20 (22)cm from cast-on edge. Bind off loosely.

RIGHT FRONT

Using size 2 (2.75mm) needles, cast on 35 (39) sts and work in k2, p2 rib, beginning first row with k3, for ¾"/2cm.

Next row Switch to size 3 (3.25mm) needles and fancy pat st, decreasing 4 (5) times evenly over the course of the row—31 (34) sts. Cont in pat st until right front measures 4¼ (4¾)"/11 (12)cm from cast-on edge. Beg with next RS row, shape neck as follows:

With RS facing, k1, k2tog, work to end; rep this dec every 2 rows 5 (6) times, then every 4 rows 6 (7) times, and, AT THE SAME TIME, shape armhole by binding off 6 sts at beg of next WS row. You will have 13 (14) sts remaining after final dec. Cont straight in pattern until right front measures 8 (8¾)"/20 (22)cm from cast-on edge. Bind off loosely. For the left front, cast on and work as for right, reversing the shaping and decreasing at neck edge as follows: Work until 3 sts remain, SKP, k1.

FINISHING

Sew up the shoulder seams. Insert a sleeve into each armhole and sew the side and sleeve seams. Using size 2 (2.75mm) needles, beg at lower right front with RS facing, pick up and knit 164 (172) sts up the right front, around the neck, and down the left front. Work in k2, p2 rib, beg and end first row with k3, for 1 row. **Next row** Form buttonholes on left front as follows: Work 3 sts in rib pat, yo, k2tog, *work 14 (16) sts in rib, yo, k2tog *, rep once from * to *, work in rib to end. Cont in rib for a total of 6 rows.

Next row Bind off loosely in rib. Sew buttons to the right front, opposite the buttonholes.

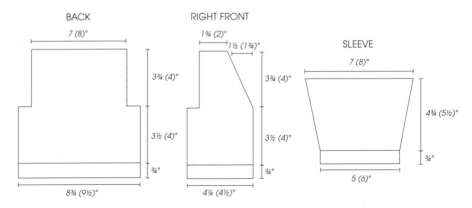

BACK
7 (8)"
3¾ (4)"
3½ (4)"
¾"
8¾ (9½)"

RIGHT FRONT
1¾ (2)"
1½ (1¾)"
3¾ (4)"
3½ (4)"
¾"
4¼ (4½)"

SLEEVE
7 (8)"
4¾ (5½)"
¾"
5 (6)"

Little eskimo

I'll be as snug as a bug in my hooded poncho and matching booties.

PONCHO

SIZES
Newborn (3 months)

MATERIALS
❋ 2 (3) 5oz/140g skeins (each approx 153yd/140m) of Lion Brand Yarn Wool-Ease Chunky (acrylic/wool) in #630-155 Silver Grey (5)

❋ 1 (1) 3oz/85g skein (approx 197yd/180m) of Lion Brand Yarn Wool-Ease (acrylic/wool) in #620-102 Ranch Red (4)

❋ 1 pair size 10 (6mm) needles

❋ Five ½"/12mm buttons

❋ Tapestry needle for the embroidery

STITCHES USED
❋ stockinette stitch
❋ seed stitch
❋ single dec (SKP)
❋ double dec (SK2P)
❋ embroidery: straight stitch

GAUGE
❋ 14 sts and 22 rows to 4"/10cm over St st using size 10 (6mm) needles and Lion Brand Yarn Wool-Ease Chunky.
Take time to check gauge.

BACK

Make the poncho in a single piece, beg at front.

Using Silver Grey, cast on 59 (63) sts, work in seed st for 2 rows, then cont as follows: 11 sts in seed st, 37 (41) sts in St st, 11 sts in seed st. Cont as established until front measures 6 (7½)"/15 (19)cm from cast-on edge.

Next row Work 28 (30) sts in pat, turn the work; place the remaining 31 (33) sts on a stitch holder while you cont on the left front. Next row Cast on 3 sts for the placket—31 (33) sts. Cont straight until left front measures 10 (11½)"/25 (29)cm from cast-on edge, ending with a RS row. Shape the neck, beg with next row:

Next row With WS facing, bind off 4 (5) sts, work to end. Work 1 row straight.

Next row Bind off 1 st, work to end. Rep the last 2 rows 2 (3) times—24 sts. Cont straight until left front measures 11 (12½)"/28 (32)cm from cast-on edge, ending with a WS row. Place these sts on a stitch holder.

Work across the 31 (33) right front sts from the stitch holder and cont straight for 1¼"/3cm, ending with a WS row.

Next row For a buttonhole, k2, k2tog, yo, work to end. Rep this buttonhole row every 1¼"/3cm twice more—3 buttonholes. Cont straight until right front measures 10 (11½)"/25 (29)cm from cast-on edge, ending with a WS row. Shape the neck, beg with next row:

Next row With RS facing, bind off 4 (5) sts, work to end. Work 1 row straight.

Next row Bind off 1 st, work to end. Rep the last 2 rows 2 (3) times—24 sts. Cont straight until left front measures 11 (12½)"/28 (32)cm from cast-on edge, ending with a WS row. Work across the 24 sts for the left front, cast on 11 (15) sts for back neck, then work across the remaining 24 sts—59 (63) sts. Cont straight until poncho measures 21¼ (24½)"/54 (62) cm from cast-on edge. Beg with next row, work in seed st for ¾"/2cm.

Next row Bind off loosely.

HOOD
Using Silver Grey, cast on 58 (60) sts and work in St st until hood measures 5 (6)"/13 (15)cm from cast-on edge. Bind off 5 (4) sts at beg of next 10 (12) rows—8 (12) sts.

Next row Bind off remaining sts.

BACK

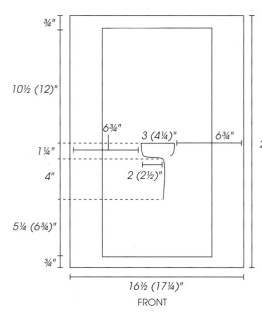

¾"

10½ (12)"

6¾"

3 (4¼)"

6¾"

1¼"

22 (25)"

2 (2½)"

4"

5¼ (6¾)"

¾"

16½ (17¼)"

FRONT

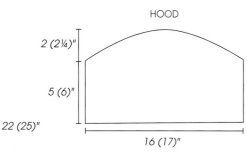

HOOD

2 (2¼)"

5 (6)"

16 (17)"

TASSEL

Cut a piece of stiff cardboard 3"/8cm wide and wind the red yarn around it about 60 times. Pass a length of yarn between the yarn and the cardboard and tie it tightly. Cut the yarn loops, then tie another length of yarn tightly 1¼"/3cm from the other end.

FINISHING

Sew up the hood seam and slip stitch the hood to the neck edge. Slip stitch the bottom of the placket and sew the buttons to the left placket, opposite the buttonholes. Using Red and a tapestry needle, embroider a row of diagonal straight sts across back and front, just above the seed st border. Attach the pompom to the peak of the hood.

BOOTIES

Using Silver Grey, cast on 23 (25) sts and work in St st as follows: *k1, inc 1, k 10 (11), inc 1, k1, inc 1, k 10 (11), inc 1, k1 *. Work 1 row straight.

Next row Rep from * to *, working the inc sts on either side of the 10 (11) sts and thus working additional sts to account for the previous inc—31 (33) sts. Work 6 rows straight, then dec beg with next row as follows:

Row 1 K10 (11), * SKP *, rep once from * to *, SK2P, k2tog, k2tog, k 10 (11).

Row 2 Purl.

Row 3 K9 (10), SKP, SK2P, k2tog, k 9 (10).

Row 4 Purl. Beg with next row, for button tab, work 21 (23) sts, cast on 3 sts, and work in seed st—24 (26) sts.

Next row For buttonhole, work 2 sts in pat, yo, k2tog, work in pat to end. Cont in seed st for 4 more rows. Bind off loosely. Using Red and the tapestry needle, embroider a row of diagonal straight sts just below the first dec row. Sew up the bootie seam and attach a button to the anklet, opposite the buttonhole tab.

Make another identical bootie, but reverse the position of the buttonhole tab.

59

Hooded car coat

Shall we go for a drive in the country?

SIZES

Newborn (3 months)

MATERIALS

❋ *4 (5) 1¾ oz/50g skeins
  (each approx 87yd/80m)
  of Bergère de France
  Magic+ (superwash
  wool/acrylic) in Abysse
  (Light Blue)* (4)
❋ *1 pair each
  size 7 (4.5mm) and
  9 (5mm) needles*
❋ *Four 1"/25mm toggle
  buttons*
❋ *Tapestry needle for the
  embroidery*

STITCHES USED

❋ *stockinette stitch*
❋ *k3, p3 rib*

GAUGES

❋ *21 sts and 24 rows to
  4"/10cm over k3, p3 rib
  using size 7 (4.5mm)
  needles.*
❋ *17 sts and 22 rows to
  4"/10cm over St st using
  size 8 (5mm) needles.
  Take time to check gauge.*

BACK

Using size 7 (4.5mm) needles, cast on 55 (61) sts and work in k3, p3 rib, beg and end row 1 with p2. Cont straight until back measures 5½ (6¼)"/14 (16)cm from cast-on edge, then shape armholes as follows:

Bind off 7 sts at beg of next row twice—41 (47) sts. Cont in k3, p3 rib until back measures 10¼ (11½)"/26 (29)cm from cast-on edge. Bind off remaining sts.

RIGHT FRONT

Using size 7 (4.5mm) needles, cast on 30 (36) sts and work in k3, p3 rib, beg row 1 with k4 and end with p2. Cont straight until right front measures 5½ (6¼)"/14 (16)cm, ending with a RS row, then shape armhole. With WS facing, bind off 7 sts at beg of next row. Cont straight until right front measures 8¾ (9½)"/22 (24)cm from cast-on edge, ending with a WS row, then shape neck.

Next row Bind off 6 (7) sts, work in rib to end. Work 1 row straight.

Next row Bind off 4 (5) sts, work in rib to end. Work 1 row straight.

Next row Bind off 2 (3) sts, work in rib to end. *Work 1 row straight.

Next row Bind off 1 st, work in rib to end *. For larger size only, rep from * to *—10 (12) sts. Cont straight until right front measures 10¼ (11½)"/26 (29)cm, ending with a RS row. Bind off remaining sts.

For left front, cast on and work as for right, forming 4 buttonholes as follows when left front measures 3½ (4¼)"/9 (11)cm from cast-on edge: With RS facing, work 4 sts in rib pat, yo, k2tog, work in rib to end. Rep this buttonhole row every 1¾"/4cm 3 times.

SLEEVES

Using size 7 (4.5mm) needles, cast on 25 (29) sts and work in k3, p3 rib, beg and end row 1 with k2 (k1). Cont in rib pat until sleeve measures 1¾"/4cm from cast-on edge.

Next row Switch to size 8 (5mm) needles and St st, work straight.

Next row K1, inc 1, work until 1 st remains, inc 1, k1. Rep this inc row every 2 rows 3 (1) times and every 4 rows 4 (6) times—41 (45) sts. Cont straight until sleeve measures 7 (8)"/18 (20)cm from cast-on edge. Bind off loosely.

HOOD

Using size 8 (5mm) needles, cast on 68 (72) sts and work in St st until hood measures 6 (6¼)"/15 (16)cm from cast-on edge. For smaller size, bind off 5 sts at beg of next 12 rows; for larger size, bind off 5 sts at beg of next 8 rows and bind off 6 sts at beg of foll 4 rows—8 sts.

Next row Bind off.

FINISHING

Sew the shoulder seams. Insert a sleeve into each armhole. Sew up the side seams and sew the sleeves, working the first 1"/2cm on the outside to allow for a turned-back cuff. Sew the hood seam and slip stitch the hood to the neck. Attach the toggle to the right front, opposite the buttonholes.

BACK
7½ (8¾)"

4¾ (5¼)"

5½ (6¼)"

10¼ (11½)"

RIGHT FRONT
2 (2¼)"

2¼ (3)"

1¾ (2)"

8¾ (10)"

5½ (6¾)"

SLEEVE
9½ (10¼)"

5½ (6¼)"

1¾"

6 (6¾)"

HOOD
6 (6¼)"

15¾ (16½)"

Prep school

My little vest keeps my arms free for cuddling.

SIZES

Newborn (3 months)

MATERIALS

- *1 (1) 1¾ oz/50g skein each (approx 178yd/165m) of Berroco Comfort DK (nylon/acrylic) in #2720 Hummus (Beige), #3722 Purple, #2740 Seedling (Light Green), and #2761 Lovage (Dark Green) 3*
- *1 pair each size 2 (2.75mm) and 3 (3.25mm) needles*
- *Two ½"/12mm light green buttons*
- *One press stud*

STITCHES USED

- *stockinette stitch*
- *garter stitch*
- *fancy garter stitch: 2 rows stockinette stitch, 2 rows garter stitch*
- *single dec (SKP)*
- *double dec (SK2P)*

GAUGE

- *27 sts and 32 rows to 4"/10cm over St st using size 3 (3.25mm) needles.*

Take time to check gauge.

BACK

Using size 2 (2.75mm) needles and Purple, cast on 65 (71) sts and work in garter st as follows: 2 rows Purple, 2 rows Light Green, 2 rows Dark Green.

Next row Switch to size 3 (3.25mm) needles and Beige, and work in St st. Cont straight for 3 rows, then shape back as follows.

Next row K2, k2tog, work until 4 sts remain, SKP, k2. Rep this dec row for smaller size every 4 rows 4 times, and for larger size, every 6 rows and 4 rows alternately another 4 times—55 (61) sts. Cont straight until back measures 3 (4)"/8 (10)cm, then shape armholes. Bind off 4 sts at beg of next 2 rows.

Next row K2, k3tog, work until 5 sts remain, SK2P, k2. Work 1 row straight.

Next row K2, k2tog, work until 4 sts remain, SKP, k2. Rep the last 2 rows once—39 (45) sts. Cont straight until back measures 6¼ (7½)"/16 (19)cm from cast-on edge, then shape neck.

Next row K9 and place on a stitch holder; complete the 2 sides separately from this point. Bind off the next 21 (27) sts for the neck and work to end. Cont straight on left back until vest measures 6¾ (8)"/17 (20)cm from cast-on edge. Bind off. Work across the remaining sts and complete the right back.

RIGHT FRONT

Using size 2 (2.75mm) needles and Purple, cast on 39 (43) sts and work in garter st as follows: 2 rows Purple, 2 rows Light Green, 2 rows Dark Green.

Next row Switch to size 3 (3.25mm) needles and Beige, and work the first 5 sts in fancy garter st, then k 34 (38)—St st. Work straight for 3 rows, then shape right front as follows:

Next row Work as given until 4 sts remain, SKP, k2. For smaller size, rep this dec row every 4 rows 4 times and for larger size every 6 rows and 4 rows alternately another 4 times. Cont straight until right front measures 3 (4)"/8 (10) cm, ending with a RS row. Bind off 4 sts at beg of next row.

Next row Knit until 5 sts remain, k3tog, k2. Work 1 row straight.

Next row Work until 4 sts remain, k2tog, k2. Rep the last 2 rows once.

BACK

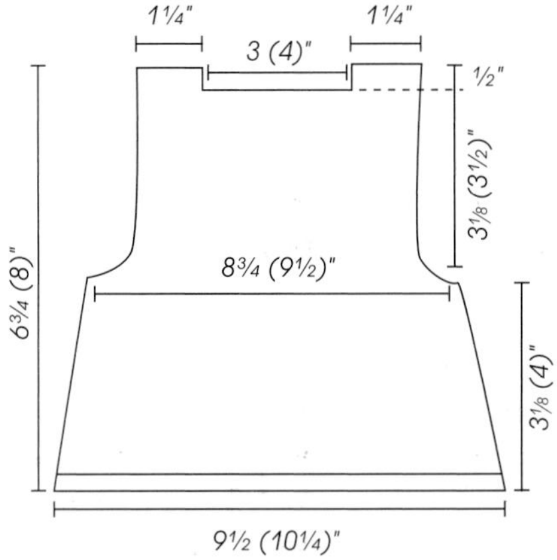
1¼"
1¼"
3 (4)"
½"
3⅛ (3½)"
6¾ (8)"
8¾ (9½)"
3⅛ (4)"
9½ (10¼)"

RIGHT FRONT

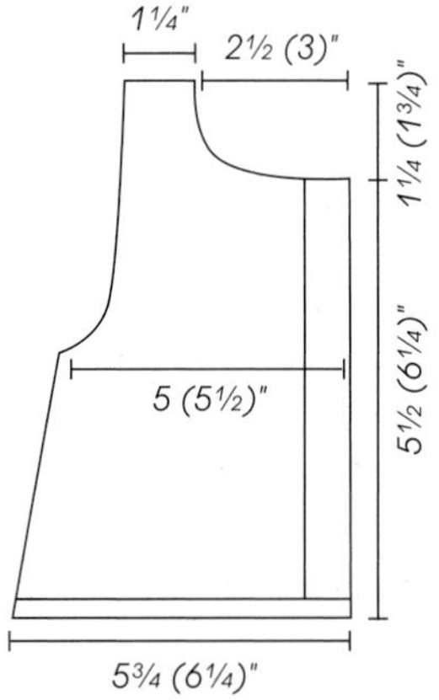
1¼"
2½ (3)"
1¼ (1¾)"
5 (5½)"
5½ (6¼)"
5¾ (6¼)"

Cont straight until right front measures 5½ (6¼)"/14 (16)cm from cast-on edge, ending with a WS row, then shape neck.
Next row Bind off 10 (12) sts, work to end. Work 1 row straight.
Next row K2 SK2P, knit to end. Rep the last 2 rows 1 (2) times. Work 1 row straight.
Next row K2, k2tog, knit to end. Rep the last 2 rows twice—9 sts. Cont straight until right front measures 6¼ (7½)"/16 (19)cm from cast-on edge, ending with a RS row.

Bind off.
For left front, cast on and work as for right, reversing the shaping and working SKP, or SK2P for neck dec.

POCKET
Using size 3 (3.25mm) needles and Purple, cast on 7 sts and work in St st as follows: Row 1 K3, inc 1, k1, inc 1, k3. Rep this row every 2 rows 4 times, always working the inc sts on either side of the central st—17

sts. Cont in St st for 2 rows, followed by garter st for 4 rows. Bind off loosely.

FINISHING
Sew the shoulder seams. Using size 2 (2.75mm) needles and Dark Green, beg at right back underarm with RS facing, pick up and knit 62 (68) sts around the armhole and work in garter st as follows: 2 rows Dark Green, 2 rows Light Green, 2 rows Purple, and, AT THE SAME TIME, dec 1

st at each end and 1 st in the middle of every 2 rows. Bind off. Repeat for left armhole, beg at left front underarm with RS facing. Using size 2 (2.75mm) needles and Dark Green, beg at right front neck with RS facing, pick up and knit 66 (82) sts around the neck and rep the same border as for armholes, decreasing 1 st even with each shoulder seam every 2 rows. Bind off. Using Beige, work 2 button loops on the right front, the first at the base of the neck and the other 1¼"/3cm lower down. Sew the side seams. Slip stitch the pocket to the right front as shown in the photo, and sew the buttons to the left front, opposite the button loops. Sew the press stud at the end of the left neck border and at the matching place on the right border.

STANDARD YARN WEIGHT SYSTEM
Categories of yarn, gauge ranges, and recommended needle and hook sizes

Yarn Weight Symbol & Category Names	0 Lace	1 Super Fine	2 Fine	3 Light	4 Medium	5 Bulky	6 Super Bulky
Type of Yarns in Category	Fingering 10 count crochet thread	Sock, Fingering, Baby	Sport, Baby	DK, Light Worsted	Worsted, Afghan, Aran	Chunky, Craft, Rug	Bulky, Roving
Knit Gauge Range* in Stockinette Stitch to 4 inches	33–40** sts	27–32 sts	23–26 sts	21–24 sts	16–20 sts	12–15 sts	6–11 sts
Recommended Needle in Metric Size Range	1.5–2.25 mm	2.25–3.25 mm	3.25–3.75 mm	3.75–4.5 mm	4.5–5.5 mm	5.5–8 mm	8 mm and larger
Recommended Needle U.S. Size Range	000 to 1	1 to 3	3 to 5	5 to 7	7 to 9	9 to 11	11 and larger
Crochet Gauge* Ranges in Single Crochet to 4 inch	32–42 double crochets**	21–32 sts	16–20 sts	12–17 sts	11–14 sts	8–11 sts	5–9 sts
Recommended Hook in Metric Size Range	Steel*** 1.6–1.4mm Regular hook 2.25 mm	2.25–3.5 mm	3.5–4.5 mm	4.5–5.5 mm	5.5–6.5 mm	6.5–9 mm	9 mm and larger
Recommended Hook U.S. Size Range	Steel*** 6, 7, 8 Regular hook B-1	B-1 to E-4	E-4 to 7	7 to I-9	I-9 to K-10½	K-10½ to M-13	M-13 and larger

*GUIDELINES ONLY: The above reflect the most commonly used gauges and needle or hook sizes for specific yarn categories. **Lace weight yarns are usually knitted or crocheted on larger needles and hooks to create lacy, openwork patterns. Accordingly, a gauge range is difficult to determine. Always follow the gauge stated in your pattern. ***Steel crochet hooks are sized differently from regular hooks—the higher the number, the smaller the hook, which is the reverse of regular hook sizing. This Standards & Guidelines booklet and downloadable symbol artwork are available at YarnStandards.com